AUGUSTE COMTE AND POSITIVISM
BY
JOHN STUART MILL

1865

PART I.
THE COURS DE PHILOSOPHIE POSITIVE.

For some time much has been said, in England and on the Continent, concerning "Positivism" and "the Positive Philosophy." Those phrases, which during the life of the eminent thinker who introduced them had made their way into no writings or discussions but those of his very few direct disciples, have emerged from the depths and manifested themselves on the surface of the philosophy of the age. It is not very widely known what they represent, but it is understood that they represent something. They are symbols of a recognised mode of thought, and one of sufficient importance to induce almost all who now discuss the great problems of philosophy, or survey from any elevated point of view the opinions of the age, to take what is termed the Positivist view of things into serious consideration, and define their own position, more or less friendly or hostile, in regard to it. Indeed, though the mode of thought expressed by the terms Positive and Positivism is widely spread, the words themselves are, as usual, better known through the enemies of that mode of thinking than through its friends; and more than one thinker who never called himself or his opinions by those appellations, and carefully guarded himself against being confounded with those who did, finds himself, sometimes to his displeasure, though generally by a tolerably correct instinct, classed with Positivists, and assailed as a Positivist. This change in the bearings of philosophic opinion commenced in England earlier than in France, where a philosophy of a contrary kind had been more widely cultivated, and had taken a firmer hold on the speculative minds of a generation formed by Royer-Collard, Cousin, Jouffroy, and their compeers. The great treatise of M. Comte was scarcely mentioned in French literature or criticism, when it was already working powerfully on the minds of many British students and thinkers. But, agreeably to the usual course of things in France, the new tendency, when it set in, set in more strongly. Those who call themselves Positivists are indeed not numerous; but all French writers who adhere to the common philosophy, now feel it necessary to begin by fortifying their position against "the Positivist school." And the mode of thinking thus designated is already manifesting its importance by one of the most unequivocal signs, the appearance of thinkers who attempt a compromise or *juste milieu* between it and its opposite. The acute critic and metaphysician M. Taine, and the distinguished chemist M. Berthelot, are the authors of the two most conspicuous of these attempts.

The time, therefore, seems to have come, when every philosophic thinker not only ought to form, but may usefully express, a judgment respecting this intellectual movement; endeavouring to understand what it is, whether it is essentially a wholesome movement, and if so, what is to be accepted and what rejected of the direction given to it by its most important movers. There cannot be a more appropriate mode of discussing these points than in the form of a critical examination of the philosophy of Auguste Comte; for which the appearance of a new edition of his fundamental treatise, with a preface by the most eminent, in every point of view, of his professed disciples, M. Littré, affords a good opportunity. The name of M. Comte is more identified than any other with this mode of thought. He is the first who has attempted its complete systematization, and the scientific extension of it to all objects of human knowledge. And in doing this he has displayed a quantity and quality of mental power, and achieved an amount of success, which have not only won but retained the high admiration of thinkers as radically and strenuously opposed as it is possible to be, to nearly the whole of his later tendencies, and to many of his earlier opinions. It would have been a mistake had such thinkers busied themselves in the first instance with drawing attention to what they regarded as errors in his great work. Until it had taken the place in the world of thought which belonged to it, the important matter was not to criticise it, but to help in making it known. To have put those who neither knew nor were capable of appreciating the greatness of the book, in possession of its vulnerable points, would have indefinitely retarded its progress to a just estimation, and was not needful for guarding against any serious inconvenience. While a writer has few readers, and no influence except on independent thinkers, the only thing worth considering in him is what he can teach us: if there be anything in which he is less wise than we are already, it may be left unnoticed until the time comes when his errors can do harm. But the high place which M. Comte has now assumed among European thinkers, and the increasing influence of his principal work, while they make it a more hopeful task than before to impress and enforce the strong points of his philosophy, have rendered it, for the first time, not inopportune to discuss his mistakes. Whatever errors he may have fallen into are now in a position to be injurious, while the free exposure of them can no longer be so.

We propose, then, to pass in review the main principles of M. Comte's philosophy; commencing with the great treatise by which, in this country, he is chiefly known, and postponing consideration of the writings of the last ten years of his life, except for the occasional illustration of detached points.

When we extend our examination to these later productions, we shall have, in the main, to reverse our judgment. Instead of recognizing, as in the Cours de Philosophic Positive, an essentially sound view of philosophy, with a few capital errors, it is in their general character that we deem the subsequent speculations false and misleading, while in the midst of this wrong general tendency, we find a crowd of valuable thoughts, and suggestions of thought, in detail. For the present we put out of the question this signal anomaly in M.

4

Comte's intellectual career. We shall consider only the principal gift which he has left to the world, his clear, full, and comprehensive exposition, and in part creation, of what he terms the Positive Philosophy: endeavouring to sever what in our estimation is true, from the much less which is erroneous, in that philosophy as he conceived it, and distinguishing, as we proceed, the part which is specially his, from that which belongs to the philosophy of the age, and is the common inheritance of thinkers. This last discrimination has been partially made in a late pamphlet, by Mr Herbert Spencer, in vindication of his own independence of thought: but this does not diminish the utility of doing it, with a less limited purpose, here; especially as Mr Spencer rejects nearly all which properly belongs to M. Comte, and in his abridged mode of statement does scanty justice to what he rejects. The separation is not difficult, even on the direct evidence given by M. Comte himself, who, far from claiming any originality not really belonging to him, was eager to connect his own most original thoughts with every germ of anything similar which he observed in previous thinkers.

The fundamental doctrine of a true philosophy, according to M. Comte, and the character by which he defines Positive Philosophy, is the following:—We have no knowledge of anything but Phaenomena; and our knowledge of phaenomena is relative, not absolute. We know not the essence, nor the real mode of production, of any fact, but only its relations to other facts in the way of succession or of similitude. These relations are constant; that is, always the same in the same circumstances. The constant resemblances which link phaenomena together, and the constant sequences which unite them as antecedent and consequent, are termed their laws. The laws of phaenomena are all we know respecting them. Their essential nature, and their ultimate causes, either efficient or final, are unknown and inscrutable to us.

M. Comte claims no originality for this conception of human knowledge. He avows that it has been virtually acted on from the earliest period by all who have made any real contribution to science, and became distinctly present to the minds of speculative men from the time of Bacon, Descartes, and Galileo, whom he regards as collectively the founders of the Positive Philosophy. As he says, the knowledge which mankind, even in the earliest ages, chiefly pursued, being that which they most needed, was *fore*knowledge: "savoir, pour prevoir." When they sought for the cause, it was mainly in order to control the effect or if it was uncontrollable, to foreknow and adapt their conduct to it. Now, all foresight of phaenomena, and power over them, depend on knowledge of their sequences, and not upon any notion we may have formed respecting their origin or inmost nature. We foresee a fact or event by means of facts which are signs of it, because experience has shown them to be its antecedents. We bring about any fact, other than our own muscular contractions, by means of some fact which experience has shown to be followed by it. All foresight, therefore, and all intelligent action, have only been possible in proportion as men have successfully attempted to ascertain the successions of phaenomena. Neither foreknowledge, nor the knowledge which is practical power, can be acquired by any other means.

The conviction, however, that knowledge of the successions and co-existences of phaenomena is the sole knowledge accessible to us, could not be arrived at in a very early stage of the progress of thought. Men have not even now left off hoping for other knowledge, nor believing that they have attained it; and that, when attained, it is, in some undefinable manner, greatly more precious than mere knowledge of sequences and co-existences. The true doctrine was not seen in its full clearness even by Bacon, though it is the result to which all his speculations tend: still less by Descartes. It was, however, correctly apprehended by Newton.[1]

But it was probably first conceived in its entire generality by Hume, who carries it a step further than Comte, maintaining not merely that the only causes of phaenomena which can be known to us are other phaenomena, their invariable antecedents, but that there is no other kind of causes: cause, as he interprets it, *means* the invariable antecedent. This is the only part of Hume's doctrine which was contested by his great adversary, Kant; who, maintaining as strenuously as Comte that we know nothing of Things in themselves, of Noumena, of real Substances and real Causes, yet peremptorily asserted their existence. But neither does Comte question this: on the contrary, all his language implies it. Among the direct successors of Hume, the writer who has best stated and defended Comte's fundamental doctrine is Dr Thomas Brown. The doctrine and spirit of Brown's philosophy are entirely Positivist, and no better introduction to Positivism than the early part of his Lectures has yet been produced. Of living thinkers we do not speak; but the same great truth formed the groundwork of all the speculative philosophy of Bentham, and pre-eminently of James Mill: and Sir William Hamilton's famous doctrine of the Relativity of human knowledge has guided many to it, though we cannot credit Sir William Hamilton himself with having understood the principle, or been willing to assent to it if he had.

The foundation of M. Comte's philosophy is thus in no way peculiar to him, but the general property of the age, however far as yet from being universally accepted even by thoughtful minds.

The philosophy called Positive is not a recent invention of M. Comte, but a simple adherence to the traditions of all the great scientific minds whose discoveries have made the human race what it is. M. Comte has never presented it in any other light. But he has made the doctrine his own by his manner of treating it. To know rightly what a thing is, we require to know, with equal distinctness, what it is not. To enter into the real character of any mode of thought, we must understand what other modes of thought compete

6

with it. M. Comte has taken care that we should do so. The modes of philosophizing which, according to him, dispute ascendancy with the Positive, are two in number, both of them anterior to it in date; the Theological, and the Metaphysical.

We use the words Theological, Metaphysical, and Positive, because they are chosen by M. Comte as a vehicle for M. Comte's ideas. Any philosopher whose thoughts another person undertakes to set forth, has a right to require that it should be done by means of his own nomenclature. They are not, however, the terms we should ourselves choose. In all languages, but especially in English, they excite ideas other than those intended. The words Positive and Positivism, in the meaning assigned to them, are ill fitted to take, root in English soil; while Metaphysical suggests, and suggested even to M. Comte, much that in no way deserves to be included in his denunciation. The term Theological is less wide of the mark, though the use of it as a term of condemnation implies, as we shall see, a greater reach of negation than need be included in the Positive creed. Instead of the Theological we should prefer to speak of the Personal, or Volitional explanation of nature; instead of Metaphysical, the Abstractional or Ontological: and the meaning of Positive would be less ambiguously expressed in the objective aspect by Phaenomenal, in the subjective by Experiential. But M. Comte's opinions are best stated in his own phraseology; several of them, indeed, can scarcely be presented in some of their bearings without it.

The Theological, which is the original and spontaneous form of thought, regards the facts of the universe as governed not by invariable laws of sequence, but by single and direct volitions of beings, real or imaginary, possessed of life and intelligence. In the infantile state of reason and experience, individual objects are looked upon as animated. The next step is the conception of invisible beings, each of whom superintends and governs an entire class of objects or events. The last merges this multitude of divinities in a single God, who made the whole universe in the beginning, and guides and carries on its phaenomena by his continued   or, as others think, only modifies them from time to time by special

The mode of thought which M. Comte terms Me   ts for phaenomena by ascribing them, not to volitions either s   but to realized abstractions. In this stage it is no longer a god   directs each of the various agencies of nature: it is a power, or a   occult quality, considered as real existences, inherent in but distinct from   he concrete bodies in which they reside, and which they in a manner animate. Instead of Dryads presiding over trees, producing and regulating their phaenomena, every plant or animal has now a Vegetative Soul, the θρεπτικὴ ψυχή of Aristotle. At a later period the Vegetative Soul has become a Plastic Force, and still later, a Vital Principle. Objects now do all that they do because

7

it is their Essence to do so, or by reason of an inherent Virtue. Phaenomena are accounted for by supposed tendencies and propensities of the abstraction Nature; which, though regarded as impersonal, is figured as acting on a sort of motives, and in a manner more or less analogous to that of conscious beings. Aristotle affirms a tendency of nature towards the best, which helps him to a theory of many natural phaenomena. The rise of water in a pump is attributed to Nature's horror of a vacuum. The fall of heavy bodies, and the ascent of flame and smoke, are construed as attempts of each to get to its *natural* place. Many important consequences are deduced from the doctrine that Nature has no breaks (non habet saltum). In medicine the curative force (vis medicatrix) of Nature furnishes the explanation of the reparative processes which modern physiologists refer each to its own particular agencies and laws.

Examples are not necessary to prove to those who are acquainted with the past phases of human thought, how great a place both the theological and the metaphysical interpretations of phaenomena have historically occupied, as well in the speculations of thinkers as in the familiar conceptions of the multitude. Many had perceived before M. Comte that neither of these modes of explanation was final: the warfare against both of them could scarcely be carried on more vigorously than it already was, early in the seventeenth century, by Hobbes. Nor is it unknown to any one who has followed the history of the various physical sciences, that the positive explanation of facts has substituted itself, step by step, for the theological and metaphysical, as the progress of inquiry brought to light an increasing number of the invariable laws of phaenomena. In these respects M. Comte has not originated anything, but has taken his place in a fight long since engaged, and on the side already in the main victorious. The generalization which belongs to himself, and in which he had not, to the best of our knowledge, been at all anticipated, is, that every distinct class of human conceptions passes through all these stages, beginning with the theological, and proceeding through the metaphysical to the positive: the metaphysical being a mere state of transition, but an indispensable one, from the theological mode of thought to the positive, which is destined finally to prevail, by the universal recognition that all phaemomena without exception are governed by invariable laws, with which no volitions, either natural or supernatural, interfere. This general theorem is completed by the addition, that the theological mode of thought has three stages, Fetichism, Polytheism, and Monotheism: the successive transitions being prepared, and indeed caused, by the gradual uprising of the two rival modes of thought, the metaphysical and the positive, and in their turn preparing the way for the ascendancy of these; first and temporarily of the metaphysical, finally of the positive.

This generalization is the most fundamental of the doctrines which originated with M. Comte; and the survey of history, which occupies the two largest volumes of the six composing his work, is a continuous exemplification and verification of the law. How well it accords with the facts, and how vast a number of the greater historical phaenomena it explains, is known only to those who have studied its exposition, where alone it can be found—in these most striking and instructive volumes. As this theory is the key to M. Comte's other generalizations, all of which are more or less dependent on it; as it forms the backbone, if we may so speak, of his philosophy, and, unless it be true, he has accomplished little; we cannot better employ part of our space than in clearing it from misconception, and giving the explanations necessary to remove the obstacles which prevent many competent persons from assenting to it.

It is proper to begin by relieving the doctrine from a religious prejudice. The doctrine condemns all theological explanations, and replaces them, or thinks them destined to be replaced, by theories which take no account of anything but an ascertained order of phaenomena. It is inferred that if this change were completely accomplished, mankind would cease to refer the constitution of Nature to an intelligent will or to believe at all in a Creator and supreme Governor of the world. This supposition is the more natural, as M. Comte was avowedly of that opinion. He indeed disclaimed, with some acrimony, dogmatic atheism, and even says (in a later work, but the earliest contains nothing at variance with it) that the hypothesis of design has much greater verisimilitude than that of a blind mechanism. But conjecture, founded on analogy, did not seem to him a basis to rest a theory on, in a mature state of human intelligence. He deemed all real knowledge of a commencement inaccessible to us, and the inquiry into it an overpassing of the essential limits of our mental faculties. To this point, however, those who accept his theory of the progressive stages of opinion are not obliged to follow him. The Positive mode of thought is not necessarily a denial of the supernatural; it merely throws back that question to the origin of all things. If the universe had a beginning, its beginning, by the very conditions of the case, was supernatural; the laws of nature cannot account for their own origin. The Positive philosopher is free to form his opinion on the subject, according to the weight he attaches to the analogies which are called marks of design, and to the general traditions of the human race. The value of these evidences is indeed a question for Positive philosophy, but it is not one upon which Positive philosophers must necessarily be agreed. It is one of M. Comte's mistakes that he never allows of open questions. Positive Philosophy maintains that within the existing order of the universe, or rather of the part of it known to us, the direct determining cause of every phaenomenon is not supernatural but natural. It is compatible with this to believe, that the universe was created, and even that it is continuously governed, by an Intelligence, provided we admit that the intelligent Governor adheres to fixed laws, which are only modified or counteracted by other laws of the same dispensation, and are never either capriciously or providentially departed from. Whoever regards all events as parts of a constant order, each one being the invariable consequent of some antecedent condition, or combination of conditions, accepts fully the Positive mode of thought: whether he acknowledges or not an universal antecedent on which the whole system of nature was originally consequent, and whether that universal antecedent is conceived as an Intelligence or not.

There is a corresponding misconception to be corrected respecting the Metaphysical mode of thought. In repudiating metaphysics, M. Comte did not interdict himself from analysing or criticising any of the abstract conceptions of the mind. He was not ignorant (though he sometimes seemed to forget) that such analysis and criticism are a necessary part of the scientific process, and accompany the scientific mind in all its operations. What he condemned was the habit of conceiving these mental abstractions as real entities, which could exert power, produce phaenomena, and the enunciation of which could be regarded as a theory or explanation of facts. Men of the present day with difficulty believe that so absurd a notion was ever really entertained, so repugnant is it to the mental habits formed by long and assiduous cultivation of the positive sciences. But those sciences, however widely cultivated, have never formed the basis of intellectual education in any society. It is with philosophy as with religion: men marvel at the absurdity of other people's tenets, while exactly parallel absurdities remain in their own, and the same man is unaffectedly astonished that words can be mistaken for things, who is treating other words as if they were things every time he opens his mouth to discuss. No one, unless entirely ignorant of the history of thought, will deny that the mistaking of abstractions for realities pervaded speculation all through antiquity and the middle ages. The mistake was generalized and systematized in the famous Ideas of Plato. The Aristotelians carried it on. Essences, quiddities, virtues residing in things, were accepted as a *bonâ fide* explanation of phaenomena. Not only abstract qualities, but the concrete names of genera and species, were mistaken for objective existences. It was believed that there were General Substances corresponding to all the familiar classes of concrete things: a substance Man, a substance Tree, a substance Animal, which, and not the individual objects so called, were directly denoted by those names. The real existence of Universal Substances was the question at issue in the famous controversy of the later middle ages between Nominalism and Realism, which is one of the turning points in the history of thought, being its first struggle to emancipate itself from the dominion of verbal abstractions. The Realists were the stronger party, but though the Nominalists for a time succumbed, the doctrine they rebelled against fell, after a short interval, with the rest of the scholastic philosophy. But while universal substances and substantial forms, being the grossest kind of realized abstractions, were the soonest discarded, Essences, Virtues, and Occult Qualities long survived them, and were first completely extruded from real existence by the Cartesians. In Descartes' conception of science, all physical phaenomena were to be explained by matter and motion, that is, not by abstractions but by invariable physical laws: though his own explanations were many of them hypothetical, and turned out to be erroneous. Long after him, however, fictitious entities (as they are happily termed by Bentham) continued to be imagined as means of accounting for the more mysterious phaenomena; above all in physiology, where, under great varieties of phrase, mysterious *forces* and *principles* were the explanation, or substitute for explanation, of the phaenomena of organized beings. To modern philosophers these fictions are merely the abstract names of the classes of phaenomena which correspond to them; and it is one of the puzzles of philosophy, how mankind, after inventing a set of mere names to keep together certain combinations of ideas or images, could have so far forgotten their own act as to invest these creations of their will with objective reality, and mistake the name of a phaenomenon for its efficient cause. What was a mystery from the purely dogmatic point of view, is cleared up by the historical. These abstract words are indeed now mere names of phaenomena, but were not so in their origin. To us they denote only the phaenomena, because we have ceased to believe in what else they once designated; and the employment of them in explanation is to us evidently, as M. Comte says, the naïf reproduction of the phaenomenon as the reason for itself: but it was not so in the beginning. The metaphysical point of view was not a perversion of the positive, but a transformation of the theological. The human mind, in framing a class of objects, did not set out from the notion of a name, but from that of a divinity. The realization of abstractions was not the embodiment of a word, but the gradual disembodiment of a Fetish.

The primitive tendency or instinct of mankind is to assimilate all the agencies which they perceive in Nature, to the only one of which they are directly conscious, their own voluntary activity. Every object which seems to originate power, that is, to act without being first visibly acted upon, to communicate motion without having first received it, they suppose to possess life, consciousness, will. This first rude conception of nature can scarcely, however, have been at any time extended to all phaenomena. The simplest observation, without which the preservation of life would have been impossible, must have pointed out many uniformities in nature, many objects which, under given circumstances, acted exactly like one another: and whenever this was observed, men's natural and untutored faculties led them to form the similar objects into a class, and to think of them together: of which it was a natural consequence to refer effects, which were exactly alike, to a single will, rather than to a number of wills precisely accordant. But this single will could not be the will of the objects themselves, since they were many: it must be the will of an invisible being, apart from the objects, and ruling them from an unknown distance. This is Polytheism. We are not aware that in any tribe of savages or negroes who have been observed, Fetichism has been found totally unmixed with Polytheism, and it is probable that the two coexisted from the earliest period at which the human mind was capable of forming objects into classes. Fetichism proper gradually becomes limited to objects possessing a marked individuality. A particular mountain or river is worshipped bodily (as it is even now by the Hindoos and the South Sea Islanders) as a divinity in itself, not the mere residence of one, long after invisible gods have been imagined as rulers of all the great classes of phaenomena, even intellectual and moral, as war, love, wisdom, beauty, &c. The worship of the earth (Tellus or Pales) and of the various heavenly bodies, was prolonged into the heart of Polytheism. Every scholar knows, though *littérateurs* and men of the world do not, that in the full vigour of the Greek religion, the Sun and Moon, not a god and goddess thereof, were sacrificed to as deities—older deities than Zeus and his descendants, belonging to the earlier dynasty of the Titans (which was the mythical version of the fact that their worship was older), and these deities had a distinct set of fables or legends connected with them. The father of Phaëthon and the lover of Endymion were not Apollo and Diana, whose identification with the Sungod and the Moongoddess was a late invention. Astrolatry, which, as M. Comte observes, is the last form of Fetichism, survived the other forms, partly because its objects, being inaccessible, were not so soon discovered to be in themselves inanimate, and partly because of the persistent spontaneousness of their apparent motions.

As far as Fetichism reached, and as long as it lasted, there was no abstraction, or classification of objects, and no room consequently for the metaphysical mode of thought. But as soon as the voluntary agent, whose will governed the phaenomenon, ceased to be the physical object itself, and was removed to an invisible position, from which he or she superintended an entire class of natural agencies, it began to seem impossible that this being should exert his powerful activity from a distance, unless through the medium of something present on the spot. Through the same Natural Prejudice which made Newton unable to conceive the possibility of his own law of gravitation without a subtle ether filling up the intervening space, and through which the attraction could be communicated—from this same natural infirmity of the human mind, it seemed indispensable that the god, at a distance from the object, must act through something residing in it, which was the immediate agent, the god having imparted to the intermediate something the power whereby it influenced and directed the object. When mankind felt a need for naming these imaginary entities, they called them the *nature* of the object, or its *essence*, or *virtues* residing in it, or by many other different names. These metaphysical conceptions were regarded as intensely real, and at first as mere instruments in the hands of the appropriate deities. But the habit being acquired of ascribing not only substantive existence, but real and efficacious agency, to the abstract entities, the consequence was that when belief in the deities declined and faded away, the entities were left standing, and a semblance of explanation of phaenomena, equal to what existed before, was furnished by the entities alone, without referring them to any volitions. When things had reached this point, the metaphysical mode of thought, had completely substituted itself for the theological.

Thus did the different successive states of the human intellect, even at an early stage of its progress, overlap one another, the Fetichistic, the Polytheistic, and the Metaphysical modes of thought coexisting even in the same minds, while the belief in invariable laws, which constitutes the Positive mode of thought, was slowly winning its way beneath them all, as observation and experience disclosed in one class of phaenomena after another the laws to which they are really subject. It was this growth of positive knowledge which principally determined the next transition in the theological conception of the universe, from Polytheism to Monotheism.

It cannot be doubted that this transition took place very tardily. The conception of a unity in Nature, which would admit of attributing it to a single will, is far from being natural to man, and only finds admittance after a long period of discipline and preparation, the obvious appearances all pointing to the idea of a government by many conflicting principles. We know how high a degree both of material civilization and of moral and intellectual development preceded the conversion of the leading populations of the world to the belief in one God. The superficial observations by which Christian travellers have persuaded themselves that they found their own Monotheistic belief in some tribes of savages, have always been contradicted by more accurate knowledge: those who have read, for instance, Mr Kohl's Kitchigami, know what to think of the Great Spirit of the American Indians, who belongs to a well-defined system of Polytheism, interspersed with large remains of an original Fetichism. We have no wish to dispute the matter with those who believe that Monotheism was the primitive religion, transmitted to our race from its first parents in uninterrupted tradition. By their own acknowledgment, the tradition was lost by all the nations of the world except a small and peculiar people, in whom it was miraculously kept alive, but who were themselves continually lapsing from it, and in all the earlier parts of their history did not hold it at all in its full meaning, but admitted the real existence of other gods, though believing their own to be the most powerful, and to be the Creator of the world. A greater proof of the unnaturalness of Monotheism to the human mind before a certain period in its development, could not well be required. The highest form of Monotheism, Christianity, has persisted to the present time in giving partial satisfaction to the mental dispositions that lead to Polytheism, by admitting into its theology the thoroughly polytheistic conception of a devil. When Monotheism, after many centuries, made its way to the Greeks and Romans from the small corner of the world where it existed, we know how the notion of daemons facilitated its reception, by making it unnecessary for Christians to deny the existence of the gods previously believed in, it being sufficient to place them under the absolute power of the new God, as the gods of Olympus were already under that of Zeus, and as the local deities of all the subjugated nations had been subordinated by conquest to the divine patrons of the Roman State.

In whatever mode, natural or supernatural, we choose to account for the early Monotheism of the Hebrews, there can be no question that its reception by the Gentiles was only rendered possible by the slow preparation which the human mind had undergone from the philosophers. In the age of the Caesars nearly the whole educated and cultivated class had outgrown the polytheistic creed, and though individually liable to returns of the superstition of their childhood, were predisposed (such of them as did not reject all religion whatever) to the acknowledgment of one Supreme Providence. It is vain to object that Christianity did not find the majority of its early proselytes among the educated class: since, except in Palestine, its teachers and propagators were mainly of that class—many of them, like St Paul, well versed in the mental culture of their time; and they had evidently found no intellectual obstacle to the new doctrine in their own minds. We must not be deceived by the recrudescence, at a much later date, of a metaphysical Paganism in the Alexandrian and other philosophical schools, provoked not by attachment to Polytheism, but by distaste for the political and social ascendancy of the Christian teachers. The fact was, that Monotheism had become congenial to the cultivated mind: and a belief which has gained the cultivated minds of any society, unless put down by force, is certain, sooner or later, to reach the multitude. Indeed the multitude itself had been prepared for it, as already hinted, by the more and more complete subordination of all other deities to the supremacy of Zeus; from which the step to a single Deity, surrounded by a host of angels, and keeping in recalcitrant subjection an army of devils, was by no means difficult.

By what means, then, had the cultivated minds of the Roman Empire been educated for Monotheism? By the growth of a practical feeling of the invariability of natural laws. Monotheism had a natural adaptation to this belief, while Polytheism naturally and necessarily conflicted with it. As men could not easily, and in fact never did, suppose that beings so powerful had their power absolutely restricted, each to its special department, the will of any divinity might always be frustrated by another: and unless all their wills were in complete harmony (which would itself be the most difficult to credit of all cases of invariability, and would require beyond anything else the ascendancy of a Supreme Deity) it was impossible that the course of any of the phaenomena under their government could be invariable. But if, on the contrary, all the phaenomena of the universe were under the exclusive and uncontrollable influence of a single will, it was an admissible supposition that this will might be always consistent with itself, and might choose to conduct each class of its operations in an invariable manner. In proportion, therefore, as the invariable laws of phaenomena revealed themselves to observers, the theory which ascribed them all to one will began to grow plausible; but must still have appeared improbable until it had come to seem likely that invariability was the common rule of all nature. The Greeks and Romans at the Christian era had reached a point of advancement at which this supposition had become probable. The admirable height to which geometry had already been carried, had familiarized the educated mind with the conception of laws absolutely invariable. The logical analysis of the intellectual processes by Aristotle had shown a similar uniformity of law in the realm of mind. In the concrete external world, the most imposing phaenomena, those of the heavenly bodies, which by their power over the imagination had done most to keep up the whole system of ideas connected with supernatural agency, had been ascertained to take place in so regular an order as to admit of being predicted with a precision which to the notions of those days must have appeared perfect. And though an equal degree of regularity had not been discerned in natural phaenomena generally, even the most empirical observation had ascertained so many cases of an uniformity *almost* complete, that inquiring minds were eagerly on the look-out for further indications pointing in the same direction; and vied with one another in the formation of theories which, though hypothetical and essentially premature, it was hoped would turn out to be correct representations of invariable laws governing large classes of phaenomena. When this hope and expectation became general, they were already a great encroachment on the original domain of the theological principle. Instead of the old conception, of events regulated from day to day by the unforeseen and changeable volitions of a legion of deities, it seemed more and more probable that all the phaenomena of the universe took place according to rules which must have been planned from the beginning; by which conception the function of the gods seemed to be limited to forming the plans, and setting the machinery in motion: their subsequent office appeared to be reduced to a sinecure, or if they continued to reign, it was in the manner of constitutional kings, bound by the laws to which they had previously given their assent. Accordingly, the pretension of philosophers to explain physical phaenomena by physical causes, or to predict their occurrence, was, up to a very late period of Polytheism, regarded as a sacrilegious insult to the gods. Anaxagoras was banished for it, Aristotle had to fly for his life, and the mere unfounded suspicion of it contributed greatly to the condemnation of Socrates. We are too well acquainted with this form of the religious sentiment even now, to have any difficulty in comprehending what must have been its violence then. It was inevitable that philosophers should be anxious to get rid of at least *these* gods, and so escape from the particular fables which stood immediately in their way; accepting a notion of divine government which harmonized better with the lessons they learnt from the study of nature, and a God concerning whom no mythos, as far as they knew, had yet been invented.

Again, when the idea became prevalent that the constitution of every part of Nature had been planned from the beginning, and continued to take place as it had been planned, this was itself a striking feature of resemblance extending through all Nature, and affording a presumption that the whole was the work, not of many, but of the same hand. It must have appeared vastly more probable that there should be one indefinitely foreseeing Intelligence and immovable Will, than hundreds and thousands of such. The philosophers had not at that time the arguments which might have been grounded on universal laws not yet suspected, such as the law of gravitation and the laws of heat; but there was a multitude, obvious even to them, of analogies and homologies in natural phaenomena, which suggested unity of plan; and a still greater number were raised up by their active fancy, aided by their premature scientific theories, all of which aimed at interpreting some phaenomenon by the analogy of others supposed to be better known; assuming, indeed, a much greater similarity among the various processes of Nature, than ampler experience has since shown to exist. The theological mode of thought thus advanced from Polytheism to Monotheism through the direct influence of the Positive mode of thought, not yet aspiring to complete speculative ascendancy. But, inasmuch as the belief in the invariability of natural laws was still imperfect even in highly cultivated minds, and in the merest infancy in the uncultivated, it gave rise to the belief in one God, but not in an immovable one. For many centuries the God believed in was flexible by entreaty, was incessantly ordering the affairs of mankind by direct volitions, and continually reversing the course of nature by miraculous interpositions; and this is believed still, wherever the invariability of law has established itself in men's convictions as a general, but not as an universal truth.

In the change from Polytheism to Monotheism, the Metaphysical mode of thought contributed its part, affording great aid to the up-hill struggle which the Positive spirit had to maintain against the prevailing form, of the Theological. M. Comte, indeed, has considerably exaggerated the share of the

Metaphysical spirit in this mental revolution, since by a lax use of terms he credits the Metaphysical mode of thought with all that is due to dialectics and negative criticism—to the exposure of inconsistencies and absurdities in the received religions. But this operation is quite independent of the Metaphysical mode of thought, and was no otherwise connected with it than in being very generally carried on by the same minds (Plato is a brilliant example), since the most eminent efficiency in it does not necessarily depend on the possession of positive scientific knowledge. But the Metaphysical spirit, strictly so called, did contribute largely to the advent of Monotheism. The conception of impersonal entities, interposed between the governing deity and the phaenomena, and forming the machinery through which these are immediately produced, is not repugnant, as the theory of direct supernatural volitions is, to the belief in invariable laws. The entities not being, like the gods, framed after the exemplar of men—being neither, like them, invested with human passions, nor supposed, like them, to have power beyond the phaenomena which are the special department of each, there was no fear of offending them by the attempt to foresee and define their action, or by the supposition that it took place according to fixed laws. The popular tribunal which condemned Anaxagoras had evidently not risen to the metaphysical point of view. Hippocrates, who was concerned only with a select and instructed class, could say with impunity, speaking of what were called the god-inflicted diseases, that to his mind they were neither more nor less god-inflicted than all others. The doctrine of abstract entities was a kind of instinctive conciliation between the observed uniformity of the facts of nature, and their dependence on arbitrary volition; since it was easier to conceive a single volition as setting a machinery to work, which afterwards went on of itself, than to suppose an inflexible constancy in so capricious and changeable a thing as volition must then have appeared. But though the régime of abstractions was in strictness compatible with Polytheism, it demanded Monotheism as the condition of its free development. The received Polytheism being only the first remove from Fetichism, its gods were too closely mixed up in the daily details of phaenomena, and the habit of propitiating them and ascertaining their will before any important action of life was too inveterate, to admit, without the strongest shock to the received system, the notion that they did not habitually rule by special interpositions, but left phaenomena in all ordinary cases to the operation of the essences or peculiar natures which they had first implanted in them. Any modification of Polytheism which would have made it fully compatible with the Metaphysical conception of the world, would have been more difficult to effect than the transition to Monotheism, as Monotheism was at first conceived.

We have given, in our own way, and at some length, this important portion of M. Comte's view of the evolution of human thought, as a sample of the manner in which his theory corresponds with and interprets historical facts, and also to obviate some objections to it, grounded on an imperfect comprehension, or rather on a mere first glance. Some, for example, think the doctrine of the three successive stages of speculation and belief, inconsistent with the fact that they all three existed contemporaneously; much as if the natural succession of the hunting, the nomad, and the agricultural state could be refuted by the fact that there are still hunters and nomads. That the three states were contemporaneous, that they all began before authentic history, and still coexist, is M. Comte's express statement: as well as that the advent of the two later modes of thought was the very cause which disorganized and is gradually destroying the primitive one. The Theological mode of explaining phaenomena was once universal, with the exception, doubtless, of the familiar facts which, being even then seen to be controllable by human will, belonged already to the positive mode of thought. The first and easiest generalizations of common observation, anterior to the first traces of the scientific spirit, determined the birth of the Metaphysical mode of thought; and every further advance in the observation of nature, gradually bringing to light its invariable laws, determined a further development of the Metaphysical spirit at the expense of the Theological, this being the only medium through which the conclusions of the Positive mode of thought and the premises of the Theological could be temporarily made compatible. At a later period, when the real character of the positive laws of nature had come to be in a certain degree understood, and the theological idea had assumed, in scientific minds, its final character, that of a God governing by general laws, the positive spirit, having now no longer need of the fictitious medium of imaginary entities, set itself to the easy task of demolishing the instrument by which it had risen. But though it destroyed the actual belief in the objective reality of these abstractions, that belief has left behind it vicious tendencies of the human mind, which are still far enough from being extinguished, and which we shall presently have occasion to characterize.

The next point on which we have to touch is one of greater importance than it seems. If all human speculation had to pass through the three stages, we may presume that its different branches, having always been very unequally advanced, could not pass from one stage to another at the same time. There must have been a certain order of succession in which the different sciences would enter, first into the metaphysical, and afterwards into the purely positive stage; and this order M. Comte proceeds to investigate. The result is his remarkable conception of a scale of subordination of the sciences, being the order of the logical dependence of those which follow on those which precede. It is not at first obvious how a mere classification of the sciences can be not merely a help to their study, but itself an important part of a body of doctrine; the classification, however, is a very important part of M. Comte's philosophy.

He first distinguishes between the abstract and the concrete sciences. The abstract sciences have to do with the laws which govern the elementary facts of Nature; laws on which all phaenomena actually realized must of course depend, but which would have been equally compatible with many other combinations than those which actually come to pass. The concrete sciences, on the contrary, concern themselves only with the particular combinations of phaenomena which are found in existence. For example; the minerals which compose our planet, or are found in it, have been produced and are held together by the laws of mechanical aggregation and by those of chemical union. It is the business of the abstract sciences, Physics and Chemistry, to ascertain these laws: to discover how and under what conditions bodies may become aggregated, and what are the possible modes and results of chemical combination. The great majority of these aggregations and combinations take place, so far as we are aware, only in our laboratories; with these the concrete science, Mineralogy, has nothing to do. Its business is with those aggregates, and those chemical compounds, which form themselves, or have at some period been formed, in the natural world. Again, Physiology, the abstract science, investigates, by such means as are available to it, the general laws of organization and life. Those laws determine what living beings are possible, and maintain the existence and determine the phaenomena of those which actually exist: but they would be equally capable of maintaining in existence plants and animals very different from these. The concrete sciences, Zoology and Botany, confine themselves to species which really exist, or can be shown to have really existed: and do not concern themselves with the mode in which even these would comport themselves under all circumstances, but only under those which really take place. They set forth the actual mode of existence of plants and animals, the phaenomena which they in fact present: but they set forth all of these, and take into simultaneous consideration the whole real existence of each species, however various the ultimate laws on which it depends, and to whatever number of different abstract sciences these laws may belong. The existence of a date tree, or of a lion, is a joint result of many natural laws, physical, chemical, biological, and even astronomical. Abstract science deals with these laws separately, but considers each of them in all its aspects, all its possibilities of operation: concrete science considers them only in combination, and so far as they exist and manifest themselves in the animals or plants of which we have experience. The distinctive attributes of the two are summed up by M. Comte in the expression, that concrete science relates to Beings, or Objects, abstract science to Events.[2]

The concrete sciences are inevitably later in their development than the abstract sciences on which they depend. Not that they begin later to be studied; on the contrary, they are the earliest cultivated, since in our abstract investigations we necessarily set out from spontaneous facts. But though we may make empirical generalizations, we can form no scientific theory of concrete phaenomena until the laws which govern and explain them are first known; and those laws are the subject of the abstract sciences. In consequence, there is not one of the concrete studies (unless we count astronomy among them) which has received, up to the present time, its final scientific constitution, or can be accounted a science, except in a very loose sense, but only materials for science: partly from insufficiency of facts, but more, because the abstract sciences, except those at the very beginning of the scale, have not attained the degree of perfection necessary to render real concrete sciences possible.

Postponing, therefore, the concrete sciences, as not yet formed, but only tending towards formation, the abstract sciences remain to be classed. These, as marked out by M. Comte, are six in number; and the principle which he proposes for their classification is admirably in accordance with the conditions of our study of Nature. It might have happened that the different classes of phaenomena had depended on laws altogether distinct; that in changing from one to another subject of scientific study, the student left behind all the laws he previously knew, and passed under the dominion of a totally new set of uniformities. The sciences would then have been wholly independent of one another; each would have rested entirely on its own inductions, and if deductive at all, would have drawn its deductions from premises exclusively furnished by itself. The fact, however, is otherwise. The relation which really subsists between different kinds of phaenomena, enables the sciences to be arranged in such an order, that in travelling through them we do not pass out of the sphere of any laws, but merely take up additional ones at each step. In this order M. Comte proposes to arrange them. He classes the sciences in an ascending series, according to the degree of complexity of their phaenomena; so that each science depends on the truths of all those which precede it, with the addition of peculiar truths of its own.

Thus, the truths of number are true of all things, and depend only on their own laws; the science, therefore, of Number, consisting of Arithmetic and Algebra, may be studied without reference to any other science. The truths of Geometry presuppose the laws of Number, and a more special class of laws peculiar to extended bodies, but require no others: Geometry, therefore, can be studied independently of all sciences except that of Number.

Rational Mechanics presupposes, and depends on, the laws of number and those of extension, and along with them another set of laws, those of Equilibrium and Motion. The truths of Algebra and Geometry nowise depend on these last, and would have been true if these had happened to be the reverse of what we find them: but the phaenomena of equilibrium and motion cannot be understood, nor even stated, without assuming the laws of number and extension, such as they actually are. The phaenomena of Astronomy depend on these three classes of laws, and on the law of gravitation besides; which last has no influence on the truths of number, geometry, or mechanics. Physics (badly named in common English parlance Natural Philosophy) presupposes the three mathematical sciences, and also astronomy; since all terrestrial phaenomena are affected by influences derived from the motions of the earth and of the heavenly bodies. Chemical phaenomena depend (besides their own laws) on all the preceding, those of physics among the rest, especially on the laws of heat and electricity; physiological phaenomena, on the laws of physics and chemistry, and their own laws in addition. The phaenomena of human society obey laws of their own, but do not depend solely upon these: they depend upon all the laws of organic and animal life, together with those of inorganic nature, these last influencing society not only through their influence on life, but by determining the physical conditions under which society has to be carried on. "Chacun de ces degré's successifs exige des inductions qui lui sont propres; mais elles ne peuvent jamais devenir systématiques que sous l'impulsion déductive resultée de tous les ordres moins compliqués."[3]

Thus arranged by M. Comte in a series, of which each term represents an advance in speciality beyond the term preceding it, and (what necessarily accompanies increased speciality) an increase of complexity—a set of phaenomena determined by a more numerous combination of laws; the sciences stand in the following order: 1st, Mathematics; its three branches following one another on the same principle, Number, Geometry, Mechanics. 2nd, Astronomy. 3rd, Physics. 4th, Chemistry. 5th, Biology. 6th, Sociology, or the Social Science, the phaemomena, of which depend on, and cannot be understood without, the principal truths of all the other sciences. The subject matter and contents of these various sciences are obvious of themselves, with the exception of Physics, which is a group of sciences rather than a single science, and is again divided by M. Comte into five departments: Barology, or the science of weight; Thermology, or that of heat; Acoustics, Optics, and Electrology. These he attempts to arrange on the same principle of increasing speciality and complexity, but they hardly admit of such a scale, and M. Comte's mode of placing them varied at different periods. All the five being essentially independent of one another, he attached little importance to their order, except that barology ought to come first, as the connecting link with astronomy, and electrology last, as the transition to chemistry.

If the best classification is that which is grounded on the properties most important for our purposes, this classification will stand the test. By placing the sciences in the order of the complexity of their subject matter, it presents them in the order of their difficulty. Each science proposes to itself a more arduous inquiry than those which precede it in the series; it is therefore likely to be susceptible, even finally, of a less degree of perfection, and will certainly arrive later at the degree attainable by it. In addition to this, each science, to establish its own truths, needs those of all the sciences anterior to it. The only means, for example, by which the physiological laws of life could have been ascertained, was by distinguishing, among the multifarious and complicated facts of life, the portion which physical and chemical laws cannot account for. Only by thus isolating the effects of the peculiar organic laws, did it become possible to discover what these are. It follows that the order in which the sciences succeed one another in the series, cannot but be, in the main, the historical order of their development; and is the only order in which they can rationally be studied. For this last there is an additional reason: since the more special and complete sciences require not only the truths of the simpler and more general ones, but still more their methods. The scientific intellect, both in the individual and in the race, must learn in the move elementary studies that art of investigation and those canons of proof which are to be put in practice in the more elevated. No intellect is properly qualified for the higher part of the scale, without due practice in the lower.

Mr Herbert Spencer, in his essay entitled "The Genesis of Science," and more recently in a pamphlet on "the Classification of the Sciences," has criticised and condemned M. Comte's classification, and proposed a more elaborate one of his own: and M. Littré, in his valuable biographical and philosophical work on M. Comte ("Auguste Comte et la Philosophie Positive"), has at some length criticised the criticism. Mr Spencer is one of the small number of persons who by the solidity and encyclopedical character of their knowledge, and their power of co-ordination and concatenation, may claim to be the peers of M. Comte, and entitled to a vote in the estimation of him. But after giving to his animadversions the respectful attention due to all that comes from Mr Spencer, we cannot find that he has made out any case. It is always easy to find fault with a classification. There are a hundred possible ways of arranging any set of objects, and something may almost always be said against the best, and in favour of the worst of them. But the merits of a classification depend on the purposes to which it is instrumental. We have shown the purposes for which M. Comte's classification is intended. Mr Spencer has not shown that it is ill adapted to those purposes: and we cannot perceive that his own answers any ends equally important. His chief objection is that if the more special sciences need the truths of the more general ones, the latter also need some of those of the former, and have at times been stopped in their progress by the imperfect state of sciences which follow long after them in M. Comte's scale; so that, the dependence being mutual, there is a *consensus*, but not an ascending scale or hierarchy of the sciences. That the earlier sciences derive help from the later is undoubtedly true; it is part of M. Comte's theory, and amply exemplified in the details of his work. When he affirms that one science historically precedes another, he does not mean that the perfection of the first precedes the humblest commencement of those which follow. Mr Spencer does not distinguish between the empirical stage of the cultivation of a branch of knowledge, and the scientific stage. The commencement of every study consists in gathering together unanalyzed facts, and treasuring up such spontaneous generalizations as present themselves to natural sagacity. In this stage any branch of inquiry can be carried on independently of every other; and it is one of M. Comte's own remarks that the most complex, in a scientific point of view, of all studies, the latest in his series, the study of man as a moral and social being, since from its absorbing interest it is cultivated more or less by every one, and pre-eminently by the great practical minds, acquired at an early period a greater stock of just though unscientific observations than the more elementary sciences. It is these empirical truths that the later and more special sciences lend to the earlier; or, at most, some extremely elementary scientific truth, which happening to be easily ascertainable by direct experiment, could be made available for carrying a previous science already founded, to a higher stage of development; a re-action of the later sciences on the earlier which M. Comte not only fully recognized, but attached great importance to systematizing.[4]

But though detached truths relating to the more complex order of phaenomena may be empirically observed, and a few of them even scientifically established, contemporaneously with an early stage of some of the sciences anterior in the scale, such detached truths, as M. Littré justly remarks, do not constitute a science. What is known of a subject, only becomes a science when it is made a connected body of truth; in which the relation between the general principles and the details is definitely made out, and each particular truth can be recognized as a case of the operation of wider laws. This point of progress, at which the study passes from the preliminary state of mere preparation, into a science, cannot be reached by the more complex studies until it has been attained by the simpler ones. A certain regularity of recurrence in the celestial appearances was ascertained empirically before much progress had been made in geometry; but astronomy could no more be a science until geometry was a highly advanced one, than the rule of three could have been practised before addition and subtraction. The truths of the simpler sciences are a part of the laws to which the phaenomena of the more complex sciences conform: and are not only a necessary element in their explanation, but must be so well understood as to be traceable through complex combinations, before the special laws which co-exist and co-operate with them can be brought to light. This is all that M. Comte affirms, and enough for his purpose.[5] He no doubt occasionally indulges in more unqualified expressions than can be completely justified, regarding the logical perfection of the construction of his series, and its exact correspondence with the historical evolution of the sciences; exaggerations confined to language, and which the details of his exposition often correct. But he is sufficiently near the truth, in both respects, for every practical purpose.[6] Minor inaccuracies must often be forgiven even to great thinkers. Mr Spencer, in the very-writings in which he criticises M. Comte, affords signal instances of them.[7]

Combining the doctrines, that every science is in a less advanced state as it occupies a higher place in the ascending scale, and that all the sciences pass through the three stages, theological, metaphysical, and positive, it follows that the more special a science is, the tardier is it in effecting each transition, so that a completely positive state of an earlier science has often coincided with the metaphysical state of the one next to it, and a purely theological state of those further on. This statement correctly represents the general course of the facts, though requiring allowances in the detail. Mathematics, for example, from the very beginning of its cultivation, can hardly at any time have been in the theological state, though exhibiting many traces of the metaphysical. No one, probably, ever believed that the will of a god kept parallel lines from meeting, or made two and two equal to four; or ever prayed to the gods to make the square of the hypothenuse equal to more or less than the sum of the squares of the sides. The most devout believers have recognized in propositions of this description a class of truths independent of the devine omnipotence. Even among the truths which popular philosophy calls by the misleading name of Contingent the few which are at once exact and obvious were probably, from the very first, excepted from the theological explanation. M. Comte observes, after Adam Smith, that we are not told in any age or country of a god of Weight. It was otherwise with Astronomy: the heavenly bodies were believed not merely to be moved by gods, but to be gods themselves: and when this theory was exploded, there movements were explained by metaphysical conceptions; such as a tendency of Nature to perfection, in virtue of which these sublime bodies, being left to themselves, move in the most perfect orbit, the circle. Even Kepler was full of fancies of this description, which only terminated when Newton, by unveiling the real physical laws of the celestial motions, closed the metaphysical period of astronomical science. As M. Comte remarks, our power of foreseeing phaenomena, and our power of controlling them, are the two things which destroy the belief of their being governed by changeable wills. In the case of phaenomena which science has not yet taught us either to foresee or to control, the theological mode of thought has not ceased to operate: men still pray for rain, or for success in war, or to avert a shipwreck or a pestilence, but not to put back the stars in their courses, to abridge the time necessary for a journey, or to arrest the tides. Such vestiges of the primitive mode of thought linger in the more intricate departments of sciences which have attained a high degree of positive development. The metaphysical mode of explanation, being less antagonistic than the theological to the idea of invariable laws, is still slower in being entirely discarded. M. Comte finds remains of it in the sciences which are the most completely positive, with the single exception of astronomy, mathematics itself not being, he thinks, altogether free from them: which is not wonderful, when we see at how very recent a date mathematicians have been able to give the really positive interpretation of their own symbols.[8] We have already however had occasion to notice M. Comte's propensity to use the term metaphysical in cases containing nothing that truly answers to his definition of the word. For instance, he considers chemistry as tainted with the metaphysical mode of thought by the notion of chemical affinity. He thinks that the chemists who said that bodies combine because they have an affinity for each other, believed in a mysterious entity residing in bodies and inducing them to combine. On any other supposition, he thinks the statement could only mean that bodies combine because they combine. But it really meant more. It was the abstract expression of the doctrine, that bodies have an invariable tendency to combine with one thing in preference to another: that the tendencies of different substances to combine are fixed quantities, of which the greater always prevails over the less, so that if A detaches B from C in one case it will do so in every other; which was called having a greater attraction, or, more technically, a greater affinity for it. This was not a metaphysical theory, but a positive generalization, which accounted for a great number of facts, and would have kept its place as a law of nature, had it not been disproved by the discovery of cases in which though A detached B from C in some circumstances, C detached it from A in others, showing the law of elective chemical combination to be a less simple one than had at first been supposed. In this case, therefore, M. Comte made a mistake: and he will be found to have made many similar ones. But in the science next after chemistry, biology, the empty mode of explanation by scholastic entities, such as a plastic force, a vital principle, and the like, has been kept up even to the present day. The German physiology of the school of Oken, notwithstanding his acknowledged genius, is almost as metaphysical as Hegel, and there is in France a quite recent revival of the Animism of Stahl. These metaphysical explanations, besides their inanity, did serious harm, by directing the course of positive scientific inquiry into wrong channels. There was indeed nothing to prevent investigating the mode of action of the supposed plastic or vital force by observation and experiment; but the phrases gave currency and coherence to a false abstraction and generalization, setting inquirers to look out for one cause of complex phaenomena which undoubtedly depended on many.

According to M. Comte, chemistry entered into the positive stage with Lavoisier, in the latter half of the last century (in a subsequent treatise he places the date a generation earlier); and biology at the beginning of the present, when Bichat drew the fundamental distinction between nutritive or vegetative and properly animal life, and referred the properties of organs to the general laws of the component tissues. The most complex of all sciences, the Social, had not, he maintained, become positive at all, but was the subject of an ever-renewed and barren contest between the theological and the metaphysical modes of thought. To make this highest of the sciences positive, and thereby complete the positive character of all human speculations, was the principal aim of his labours, and he believed himself to have accomplished it in the last three volumes of his Treatise. But the term Positive is not, any more than Metaphysical, always used by M. Comte in the same meaning. There never can have been a period in any science when it was not in some degree positive, since it always professed to draw conclusions from experience and observation. M. Comte would have been the last to deny that previous to his own speculations, the world possessed a multitude of truths, of greater or less certainty, on social subjects, the evidence of which was obtained by inductive or deductive processes from observed sequences of phaenomena. Nor could it be denied that the best writers on subjects upon which so many men of the highest mental capacity had employed their powers, had accepted as thoroughly the positive point of view, and rejected the theological and metaphysical as decidedly, as M. Comte himself. Montesquieu; even Macchiavelli; Adam Smith and the political economists universally, both in France and in England; Bentham, and all thinkers initiated by him,—had a full conviction that social phaenomena conform to invariable laws, the discovery and illustration of which was their great object as speculative thinkers. All that can be said is, that those philosophers did not get so far as M. Comte in discovering the methods best adapted to bring these laws to light. It was not, therefore, reserved for M. Comte to make sociological inquiries positive. But what he really meant by making a science positive, is what we will call, with M. Littré, giving it its final scientific constitution; in other words, discovering or proving, and pursuing to their consequences, those of its truths which are fit to form the connecting links among the rest: truths which are to it what the law of gravitation is to astronomy, what the elementary properties of the tissues are to physiology, and we will add (though M. Comte did not) what the laws of association are to psychology. This is an operation which, when accomplished, puts an end to the empirical period, and enables the science to be conceived as a co-ordinated and coherent body of doctrine. This is what had not yet been done for sociology; and the hope of effecting it was, from his early years, the prompter and incentive of all M. Comte's philosophic labours.

It was with a view to this that he undertook that wonderful systematization of the philosophy of all the antecedent sciences, from mathematics to physiology, which, if he had done nothing else, would have stamped him, in all minds competent to appreciate it, as one of the principal thinkers of the age. To make its nature intelligible to those who are not acquainted with it, we must explain what we mean by the philosophy of a science, as distinguished from the science itself. The proper meaning of philosophy we take to be, what the ancients understood by it—the scientific knowledge of Man, as an intellectual, moral, and social being. Since his intellectual faculties include his knowing faculty, the science of Man includes everything that man can know, so far as regards his mode of knowing it: in other words, the whole doctrine of the conditions of human knowledge. The philosophy of a Science thus comes to mean the science itself, considered not as to its results, the truths which it ascertains, but as to the processes by which the mind attains them, the marks by which it recognises them, and the co-ordinating and methodizing of them with a view to the greatest clearness of conception and the fullest and readiest availibility for use: in one word, the logic of the science. M. Comte has accomplished this for the first five of the fundamental sciences, with a success which can hardly be too much admired. We never reopen even the least admirable part of this survey, the volume on chemistry and biology (which was behind the actual state of those sciences when first written, and is far in the rear of them now), without a renewed sense of the great reach of its speculations, and a conviction that the way to a complete rationalizing of those sciences, still very imperfectly conceived by most who cultivate them, has been shown nowhere so successfully as there.

Yet, for a correct appreciation of this great philosophical achievement, we ought to take account of what has not been accomplished, as well as of what has. Some of the chief deficiencies and infirmities of M. Comte's system of thought will be found, as is usually the case, in close connexion with its greatest successes.

The philosophy of Science consists of two principal parts; the methods of investigation, and the requisites of proof. The one points out the roads by which the human intellect arrives at conclusions, the other the mode of testing their evidence. The former if complete would be an Organon of Discovery, the latter of Proof. It is to the first of these that M. Comte principally confines himself, and he treats it with a degree of perfection hitherto unrivalled. Nowhere is there anything comparable, in its kind, to his survey of the resources which the mind has at its disposal for investigating the laws of phaenomena; the circumstances which render each of the fundamental modes of exploration suitable or unsuitable to each class of phaenomena; the extensions and transformations which the process of investigation has to undergo in adapting itself to each new province of the field of study; and the especial gifts with which every one of the fundamental sciences enriches the method of positive inquiry, each science in its turn being the best fitted to bring to perfection one process or another. These, and many cognate subjects, such as the theory of Classification, and the proper use of scientific Hypotheses, M. Comte has treated with a completeness of insight which leaves little to be desired. Not less admirable is his survey of the most comprehensive truths that had been arrived at by each science, considered as to their relation to the general sum of human knowledge, and their logical value as aids to its further progress. But after all this, there remains a further and distinct question. We are taught the right way of searching for results, but when a result has been reached, how shall we know that it is true? How assure ourselves that the process has been performed correctly, and that our premises, whether consisting of generalities or of particular facts, really prove the conclusion we have grounded on them? On this question M. Comte throws no light. He supplies no test of proof. As regards deduction, he neither recognises the syllogistic system of Aristotle and his successors (the insufficiency of which is as evident as its utility is real) nor proposes any other in lieu of it: and of induction he has no canons whatever. He does not seem to admit the possibility of any general criterion by which to decide whether a given inductive inference is correct or not. Yet he does not, with Dr Whewell, regard an inductive theory as proved if it accounts for the facts: on the contrary, he sets himself in the strongest opposition to those scientific hypotheses which, like the luminiferous ether, are not susceptible of direct proof, and are accepted on the sole evidence of their aptitude for explaining phenomena. He maintains that no hypothesis is legitimate unless it is susceptible of verification, and that none ought to be accepted as true unless it can be shown not only that it accords with the facts, but that its falsehood would be inconsistent with them. He therefore needs a test of inductive proof; and in assigning none, he seems to give up as impracticable the main problem of Logic properly so called. At the beginning of his treatise he speaks of a doctrine of Method, apart from particular applications, as conceivable, but not needful: method, according to him, is learnt only by seeing it in operation, and the logic of a science can only usefully be taught through the science itself. Towards the end of the work, he assumes a more decidedly negative tone, and treats the very conception of studying Logic otherwise than in its applications as chimerical. He got on, in his subsequent writings, to considering it as wrong. This indispensable part of Positive Philosophy he not only left to be supplied by others, but did all that depended on him to discourage them from attempting it.

This hiatus in M. Comte's system is not unconnected with a defect in his original conception of the subject matter of scientific investigation, which has been generally noticed, for it lies on the surface, and is more apt to be exaggerated than overlooked. It is often said of him that he rejects the study of causes. This is not, in the correct acceptation, true, for it is only questions of ultimate origin, and of Efficient as distinguished from what are called Physical causes, that he rejects. The causes that he regards as inaccessible are causes which are not themselves phaenomena. Like other people he admits the study of causes, in every sense in which one physical fact can be the cause of another. But he has an objection to the *word* cause; he will only consent to speak of Laws of Succession: and depriving himself of the use of a word which has a Positive meaning, he misses the meaning it expresses. He sees no difference between such generalizations as Kepler's laws, and such as the theory of gravitation. He fails to perceive the real distinction between the laws of succession and coexistence which thinkers of a different school call Laws of Phaenomena, and those of what they call the action of Causes: the former exemplified by the succession of day and night, the latter by the earth's rotation which causes it. The succession of day and night is as much an invariable sequence, as the alternate exposure of opposite sides of the earth to the sun. Yet day and night are not the causes of one another; why? Because their sequence, though invariable in our experience, is not unconditionally so: those facts only succeed each other, provided that the presence and absence of the sun succeed each other, and if this alternation were to cease, we might have either day or night unfollowed by one another. There are thus two kinds of uniformities of succession, the one unconditional, the other conditional on the first: laws of causation, and other successions dependent on those laws. All ultimate laws are laws of causation, and the only universal law beyond the pale of mathematics is the law of universal causation, namely, that every phaenomenon has a phaenomenal cause; has some phaenomenon other than itself, or some combination of phaenomena, on which it is invariably and unconditionally consequent. It is on the universality of this law that the possibility rests of establishing a canon of Induction. A general proposition inductively obtained is only then proved to be true, when the instances on which it rests are such that if they have been correctly observed, the falsity of the generalization would be inconsistent with the constancy of causation; with the universality of the fact that the phaenomena of nature take place according to invariable laws of succession.[9] It is probable, therefore, that M. Comte's determined abstinence from the word and the idea of Cause, had much to do with his inability to conceive an Inductive Logic, by diverting his attention from the only basis upon which it could be founded.

We are afraid it must also be said, though shown only by slight indications in his fundamental work, and coming out in full evidence only in his later writings—that M. Comte, at bottom, was not so solicitous about completeness of proof as becomes a positive philosopher, and that the unimpeachable objectivity, as he would have called it, of a conception—its exact correspondence to the realities of outward fact—was not, with him, an indispensable condition of adopting it, if it was subjectively useful, by affording facilities to the mind for grouping phaenomena. This appears very curiously in his chapters on the philosophy of Chemistry. He recommends, as a judicious use of "the degree of liberty left to our intelligence by the end and purpose of positive science," that we should accept as a convenient generalization the doctrine that all chemical composition is between two elements only; that every substance which our analysis decomposes, let us say into four elements, has for its immediate constituents two hypothetical substances, each compounded of two simpler ones. There would have been nothing to object to in this as a scientific hypothesis, assumed tentatively as a means of suggesting experiments by which its truth may be tested. With this for its destination, the conception, would have been legitimate and philosophical; the more so, as, if confirmed, it would have afforded an explanation of the fact that some substances which analysis shows to be composed of the same elementary substances in the same proportions, differ in their general properties, as for instance, sugar and gum.[10] And if, besides affording a reason for difference between things which differ, the hypothesis had afforded a reason for agreement between things which agree; if the intermediate link by which the quaternary compound was resolved into two binary ones, could have been so chosen as to bring each of them within the analogies of some known class of binary compounds (which it is easy to suppose possible, and which in some particular instances actually happens); [11] the universality of binary composition would have been a successful example of an hypothesis in anticipation of a positive theory, to give a direction to inquiry which might end in its being either proved or abandoned. But M. Comte evidently thought that even though it should never be proved —however many cases of chemical composition might always remain in which the theory was still as hypothetical as at first—so long as it was not actually disproved (which it is scarcely in the nature of the case that it should ever be) it would deserve to be retained, for its mere convenience in bringing a large body of phaenomena under a general conception. In a *résumé* of the general principles of the positive method at the end of the work, he claims, in express terms, an unlimited license of adopting "without any vain scruple" hypothetical conceptions of this sort; "in order to satisfy, within proper limits, our just mental inclinations, which always turn, with an instinctive predilection, towards simplicity, continuity, and generality of conceptions, while always respecting the reality of external laws in so far as accessible to us" (vi. 639). "The most philosophic point of view leads us to conceive the study of natural laws as destined to represent the external world so as to give as much satisfaction to the essential inclinations of our intelligence, as is consistent with the degree of exactitude commanded by the aggregate of our practical wants" (vi. 642). Among these "essential inclinations" he includes not only our "instinctive predilection for order and harmony," which makes us relish any conception, even fictitious, that helps to reduce phaenomena to system; but even our feelings of taste, "les convenances purement esthétiques," which, he says, have a legitimate part in the employment of the "genre de liberté" resté facultatif pour notre intelligence." After the due satisfaction of our "most eminent mental inclinations," there will still remain "a considerable margin of indeterminateness, which should be made use of to give a direct gratification to our *besoin* of ideality, by embellishing our scientific thoughts, without injury to their essential reality" (vi. 647). In consistency with all this, M. Comte warns thinkers against too severe a scrutiny of the exact truth of scientific laws, and stamps with "severe reprobation" those who break down "by too minute an investigation" generalizations already made, without being able to substitute others (vi. 639): as in the case of Lavoisier's general theory of chemistry, which would have made that science more satisfactory than at present to "the instinctive inclinations of our intelligence" if it had turned out true, but unhappily it did not. These mental dispositions in M. Comte account for his not having found or sought a logical criterion of proof; but they are scarcely consistent with his inveterate hostility to the hypothesis of the luminiferous ether, which certainly gratifies our "predilection for order and harmony," not to say our "besoin d'idéalite", in no ordinary degree. This notion of the "destination" of the study of natural laws is to our minds a complete dereliction of the essential principles which form the Positive conception of science; and contained the germ of the perversion of his own philosophy which marked his later years. It might be interesting, but scarcely worth while, to attempt to penetrate to the just thought which misled M. Comte, for there is almost always a grain of truth in the errors of an original and powerful mind. There is another grave aberration in M. Comte's view of the method of positive science, which though not more unphilosophical than the last mentioned, is of greater practical importance. He rejects totally, as an invalid process, psychological observation properly so called, or in other words, internal consciousness, at least as regards our intellectual operations. He gives no place in his series of the science of Psychology, and always speaks of it with contempt. The study of mental phaenomena, or, as he expresses it, of moral and intellectual functions, has a place in his scheme, under the head of Biology, but only as a branch of physiology. Our knowledge of the human mind must, he thinks, be acquired by observing other people. How we are to observe other people's mental operations, or how interpret the signs of them without having learnt what the signs mean by knowledge of ourselves, he does not state. But it is clear to him that we can learn very little about the feelings, and nothing at all about the intellect, by self-observation. Our intelligence can observe all other things, but not itself: we cannot observe ourselves observing, or observe ourselves reasoning: and if we could, attention to this reflex operation would annihilate its object, by stopping the process observed.

There is little need for an elaborate refutation of a fallacy respecting which the only wonder is that it should impose on any one. Two answers may be given to it. In the first place, M. Comte might be referred to experience, and to the writings of his countryman M. Cardaillac and our own Sir William Hamilton, for proof that the mind can not only be conscious of, but attend to, more than one, and even a considerable number, of impressions at once. [12] It is true that attention is weakened by being divided; and this forms a special difficulty in psychological observation, as psychologists (Sir William Hamilton in particular) have fully recognised; but a difficulty is not an impossibility. Secondly, it might have occurred to M. Comte that a fact may be studied through the medium of memory, not at the very moment of our perceiving it, but the moment after: and this is really the mode in which our best knowledge of our intellectual acts is generally acquired. We reflect on what we have been doing, when the act is past, but when its impression in the memory is still fresh. Unless in one of these ways, we could not have acquired the knowledge, which nobody denies us to have, of what passes in our minds. M. Comte would scarcely have affirmed that we are not aware of our own intellectual operations. We know of our observings and our reasonings, either at the very time, or by memory the moment after; in either case, by direct knowledge, and not (like things done by us in a state of somnambulism) merely by their results. This simple fact destroys the whole of M. Comte's argument. Whatever we are directly aware of, we can directly observe.

And what Organon for the study of "the moral and intellectual functions" does M. Comte offer, in lieu of the direct mental observation which he repudiates? We are almost ashamed to say, that it is Phrenology! Not, indeed, he says, as a science formed, but as one still to be created; for he rejects almost all the special organs imagined by phrenologists, and accepts only their general division of the brain into the three regions of the propensities, the sentiments, and the intellect,[13] and the subdivision of the latter region between the organs of meditation and those of observation. Yet this mere first outline of an apportionment of the mental functions among different organs, he regards as extricating the mental study of man from the metaphysical stage, and elevating it to the positive. The condition of mental science would be sad indeed if this were its best chance of being positive; for the later course of physiological observation and speculation has not tended to confirm, but to discredit, the phrenological hypothesis. And even if that hypothesis were true, psychological observation would still be necessary; for how is it possible to ascertain the correspondence between two things, by observation of only one of them? To establish a relation between mental functions and cerebral conformations, requires not only a parallel system of observations applied to each, but (as M. Comte himself, with some inconsistency, acknowledges) an analysis of the mental faculties, "des diverses facultés élémentaires," (iii. 573), conducted without any reference to the physical conditions, since the proof of the theory would lie in the correspondence between the division of the brain into organs and that of the mind into faculties, each shown by separate evidence. To accomplish this analysis requires direct psychological study carried to a high pitch of perfection; it being necessary, among other things, to investigate the degree in which mental character is created by circumstances, since no one supposes that cerebral conformation does all, and circumstances nothing. The phrenological study of Mind thus supposes as its necessary preparation the whole of the Association psychology. Without, then, rejecting any aid which study of the brain and nerves can afford to psychology (and it has afforded, and will yet afford, much), we may affirm that M. Comte has done nothing for the constitution of the positive method of mental science. He refused to profit by the very valuable commencements made by his predecessors, especially by Hartley, Brown, and James Mill (if indeed any of those philosophers were known to him), and left the psychological branch of the positive method, as well as psychology itself, to be put in their true position as a part of Positive Philosophy by successors who duly placed themselves at the twofold point of view of physiology and psychology, Mr Bain and Mr Herbert Spencer. This great mistake is not a mere hiatus in M. Comte's system, but the parent of serious errors in his attempt to create a Social Science. He is indeed very skilful in estimating the effect of circumstances in moulding the general character of the human race; were he not, his historical theory could be of little worth: but in appreciating the influence which circumstances exercise, through psychological laws, in producing diversities of character, collective or individual, he is sadly at fault.

After this summary view of M. Comte's conception of Positive Philosophy, it remains to give some account of his more special and equally ambitious attempt to create the Science of Sociology, or, as he expresses it, to elevate the study of social phaenomena to the positive state.

He regarded all who profess any political opinions as hitherto divided between the adherents of the theological and those of the metaphysical mode of thought: the former deducing all their doctrines from divine ordinances, the latter from abstractions. This assertion, however, cannot be intended in the same sense as when the terms are applied to the sciences of inorganic nature; for it is impossible that acts evidently proceeding from the human will could be ascribed to the agency (at least immediate) of either divinities or abstractions. No one ever regarded himself or his fellow-man as a mere piece of machinery worked by a god, or as the abode of an entity which was the true author of what the man himself appeared to do. True, it was believed that the gods, or God, could move or change human wills, as well as control their consequences, and prayers were offered to them accordingly, rather as able to overrule the spontaneous course of things, than as at each instant carrying it on. On the whole, however, the theological and metaphysical conceptions, in their application to sociology, had reference not to the production of phaenomena, but to the rule of duty, and conduct in life. It is this which was based, either on a divine will, or on abstract mental conceptions, which, by an illusion of the rational faculty, were invested with objective validity. On the one hand, the established rules of morality were everywhere referred to a divine origin. In the majority of countries the entire civil and criminal law was looked upon as revealed from above; and it is to the petty military communities which escaped this delusion, that man is indebted for being now a progressive being. The fundamental institutions of the state were almost everywhere believed to have been divinely established, and to be still, in a greater or less degree, of divine authority. The divine right of certain lines of kings to rule, and even to rule absolutely, was but lately the creed of the dominant party in most countries of Europe; while the divine right of popes and bishops to dictate men's beliefs (and not respecting the invisible world alone) is still striving, though under considerable difficulties, to rule mankind. When these opinions began to be out of date, a rival theory presented itself to take their place. There were, in truth, many such theories, and to some of them the term metaphysical, in M. Comte's sense, cannot justly be applied. All theories in which the ultimate standard of institutions and rules of action was the happiness of mankind, and observation and experience the guides (and some such there have been in all periods of free speculation), are entitled to the name Positive, whatever, in other respects, their imperfections may be. But these were a small minority. M. Comte was right in affirming that the prevailing schools of moral and political speculation, when not theological, have been metaphysical. They affirmed that moral rules, and even political institutions, were not means to an end, the general good, but corollaries evolved from the conception of Natural Rights. This was especially the case in all the countries in which the ideas of publicists were the offspring of the Roman Law. The legislators of opinion on these subjects, when not theologians, were lawyers: and the Continental lawyers followed the Roman jurists, who followed the Greek metaphysicians, in acknowledging as the ultimate source of right and wrong in morals, and consequently in institutions, the imaginary law of the imaginary being Nature. The first systematizers of morals in Christian Europe, on any other than a purely theological basis, the writers on International Law, reasoned wholly from these premises, and transmitted them to a long line of successors. This mode of thought reached its culmination in Rousseau, in whose hands it became as powerful an instrument for destroying the past, as it was impotent for directing the future. The complete victory which this philosophy gained, in speculation, over the old doctrines, was temporarily followed by an equally complete practical triumph, the French Revolution: when, having had, for the first time, a full opportunity of developing its tendencies, and showing what it could not do, it failed so conspicuously as to determine a partial reaction to the doctrines of feudalism and Catholicism. Between these and the political metaphysics (meta-politics as Coleridge called it) of the Revolution, society has since oscillated; raising up in the process a hybrid intermediate party, termed Conservative, or the party of Order, which has no doctrines of its own, but attempts to hold the scales even between the two others, borrowing alternately the arguments of each, to use as weapons against whichever of the two seems at the moment most likely to prevail.

Such, reduced to a very condensed form, is M. Comte's version of the state of European opinion on politics and society. An Englishman's criticism would be, that it describes well enough the general division of political opinion in France and the countries which follow her lead, but not in England, or the communities of English origin: in all of which, divine right died out with the Jacobites, and the law of nature and natural rights have never been favourites even with the extreme popular party, who preferred to rest their claims on the historical traditions of their own country, and on maxims drawn from its law books, and since they outgrew this standard, almost always base them on general expediency. In England, the preference of one form of government to another seldom turns on anything but the practical consequences which it produces, or which are expected from it. M. Comte can point to little of the nature of metaphysics in English politics, except "la métaphysique constitutionnelle," a name he chooses to give to the conventional fiction by which the occupant of the throne is supposed to be the source from whence all power emanates, while nothing can be further from the belief or intention of anybody than that such should really be the case. Apart from this, which is a matter of forms and words, and has no connexion with any belief except belief in the proprieties, the severest criticism can find nothing either worse or better, in the modes of thinking either of our conservative or of our liberal party, than a particularly shallow and flimsy kind of positivism. The working classes indeed, or some portion of them, perhaps still rest their claim to universal suffrage on abstract right, in addition to more substantial reasons, and thus far and no farther does metaphysics prevail in the region of English politics. But politics is not the entire art of social existence: ethics is a still deeper and more vital part of it: and in that, as much in England as elsewhere, the current opinions are still divided between the theological mode of thought and the metaphysical. What is the whole doctrine of Intuitive Morality, which reigns supreme wherever the idolatry of Scripture texts has abated and the influence of Bentham's philosophy has not reached, but the metaphysical state of ethical science? What else, indeed, is the whole *a priori* philosophy, in morals, jurisprudence, psychology, logic, even physical science, for it does not always keep its hands off that, the oldest domain of observation and experiment? It has the universal diagnostic of the metaphysical mode of thought, in the Comtean sense of the word; that of erecting a mere creation of the mind into a test or *norma* of external truth, and presenting the abstract expression of the beliefs already entertained, as the reason and evidence which justifies them. Of those who still adhere to the old opinions we need not speak; but when one of the most vigorous as well as boldest thinkers that English speculation has yet produced, full of the true scientific spirit, Mr Herbert Spencer, places in the front of his philosophy the doctrine that the ultimate test of the truth of a proposition is the inconceivableness of its negative; when, following in the steps of Mr Spencer, an able expounder of positive philosophy like Mr Lewes, in his meritorious and by no means superficial work on Aristotle, after laying, very justly, the blame of almost every error of the ancient thinkers on their neglecting to *verify* their opinions, announces that there are two kinds of verification, the Real and the Ideal, the ideal test of truth being that its negative is unthinkable, and by the application of that test judges that gravitation must be universal even in the stellar regions, because in the absence of proof to the contrary, "the idea of matter without gravity is unthinkable;"—when those from whom it was least to be expected thus set up acquired necessities of thought in the minds of one or two generations as evidence of real necessities in the universe, we must admit that the metaphysical mode of thought still rules the higher philosophy, even in the department of inorganic nature, and far more in all that relates to man as a moral, intellectual, and social being.

But, while M. Comte is so far in the right, we often, as already intimated, find him using the name metaphysical to denote certain practical conclusions, instead of a particular kind of theoretical premises. Whatever goes by the different names of the revolutionary, the radical, the democratic, the liberal, the free-thinking, the sceptical, or the negative and critical school or party in religion, politics, or philosophy, all passes with him under the designation of metaphysical, and whatever he has to say about it forms part of his description of the metaphysical school of social science. He passes in review, one after another, what he deems the leading doctrines of the revolutionary school of politics, and dismisses them all as mere instruments of attack upon the old social system, with no permanent validity as social truth.

He assigns only this humble rank to the first of all the articles of the liberal creed, "the absolute right of free examination, or the dogma of unlimited liberty of conscience." As far as this doctrine only means that opinions, and their expression, should be exempt from *legal* restraint, either in the form of prevention or of penalty, M. Comte is a firm adherent of it: but the *moral* right of every human being, however ill-prepared by the necessary instruction and discipline, to erect himself into a judge of the most intricate as well as the most important questions that can occupy the human intellect, he resolutely denies. "There is no liberty of conscience," he said in an early work, "in astronomy, in physics, in chemistry, even in physiology, in the sense that every one would think it absurd not to accept in confidence the principles established in those sciences by the competent persons. If it is otherwise in politics, the reason is merely because, the old doctrines having gone by and the new ones not being yet formed, there are not properly, during the interval, any established opinions." When first mankind outgrew the old doctrines, an appeal from doctors and teachers to the outside public was inevitable and indispensable, since without the toleration and encouragement of discussion and criticism from all quarters, it would have been impossible for any new doctrines to grow up. But in itself, the practice of carrying the questions which more than all others require special knowledge and preparation, before the incompetent tribunal of common opinion, is, he contends, radically irrational, and will and ought to cease when once mankind have again made up their minds to a system of doctrine. The prolongation of this provisional state, producing an ever-increasing divergence of opinions, is already, according to him, extremely dangerous, since it is only when there is a tolerable unanimity respecting the rule of life, that a real moral control can be established over the self-interest and passions of individuals. Besides which, when every man is encouraged to believe himself a competent judge of the most difficult social questions, he cannot be prevented from thinking himself competent also to the most important public duties, and the baneful competition for power and official functions spreads constantly downwards to a lower and lower grade of intelligence. In M. Comte's opinion, the peculiarly complicated nature of sociological studies, and the great amount of previous knowledge and intellectual discipline requisite for them, together with the serious consequences that may be produced by even, temporary errors on such subjects, render it necessary in the case of ethics and politics, still more than of mathematics and physics, that whatever legal liberty may exist of questioning and discussing, the opinions of mankind should really be formed for them by an exceedingly small number of minds of the highest class, trained to the task by the most thorough and laborious mental preparation: and that the questioning of their conclusions by any one, not of an equivalent grade of intellect and instruction, should be accounted equally presumptuous, and more blamable, than the attempts occasionally made by sciolists to refute the Newtonian astronomy. All this is, in a sense, true: but we confess our sympathy with those who feel towards it like the man in the story, who being asked whether he admitted that six and five make eleven, refused to give an answer until he knew what use was to be made of it. The doctrine is one of a class of truths which, unless completed by other truths, are so liable to perversion, that we may fairly decline to take notice of them except in connexion with some definite application. In justice to M. Comte it should be said that he does not wish this intellectual dominion to be exercised over an ignorant people. Par from him is the thought of promoting the allegiance of the mass to scientific authority by withholding from them scientific knowledge. He holds it the duty of society to bestow on every one who grows up to manhood or womanhood as complete a course of instruction in every department of science, from mathematics to sociology, as can possibly be made general: and his ideas of what is possible in that respect are carried to a length to which few are prepared to follow him. There is something startling, though, when closely looked into, not Utopian or chimerical, in the amount of positive knowledge of the most varied kind which he believes may, by good methods of teaching, be made the common inheritance of all persons with ordinary faculties who are born into the world: not the mere knowledge of results, to which, except for the practical arts, he attaches only secondary value, but knowledge also of the mode in which those results were attained, and the evidence on which they rest, so far as it can be known and understood by those who do not devote their lives to its study.

We have stated thus fully M. Comte's opinion on the most fundamental doctrine of liberalism, because it is the clue to much of his general conception of politics. If his object had only been to exemplify by that doctrine the purely negative character of the principal liberal and revolutionary schools of thought, he need not have gone so far: it would have been enough to say, that the mere liberty to hold and express any creed, cannot itself *be* that creed. Every one is free to believe and publish that two and two make ten, but the important thing is to know that they make four. M. Comte has no difficulty in making out an equally strong case against the other principal tenets of what he calls the revolutionary school; since all that they generally amount to is, that something ought not to be: which cannot possibly be the whole truth, and which M. Comte, in general, will not admit to be even part of it. Take for instance the doctrine which denies to governments any initiative in social progress, restricting them to the function of preserving order, or in other words keeping the peace: an opinion which, so far as grounded on so-called rights of the individual, he justly regards as purely metaphysical; but does not recognise that it is also widely held as an inference from the laws of human nature and human affairs, and therefore, whether true or false, as a Positive doctrine. Believing with M. Comte that there are no absolute truths in the political art, nor indeed in any art whatever, we agree with him that the *laisser faire* doctrine, stated without large qualifications, is both unpractical and unscientific; but it does not follow that those who assert it are not, nineteen times out of twenty, practically nearer the truth than those who deny it. The doctrine of Equality meets no better fate at M. Comte's hands. He regards it as the erection into an absolute dogma of a mere protest against the inequalities which came down from the middle ages, and answer no legitimate end in modern society. He observes, that mankind in a normal state, having to act together, are necessarily, in practice, organized and classed with some reference to their unequal aptitudes, natural or acquired, which demand that some should be under the direction of others: scrupulous regard being at the same time had to the fulfilment towards all, of "the claims rightfully inherent in the dignity of a human being; the aggregate of which, still very insufficiently appreciated, will constitute more and more the principle of universal morality as applied to daily use... a grand moral obligation, which has never been directly denied since the abolition of slavery" (iv. 51). There is not a word to be said against these doctrines: but the practical question is one which M. Comte never even entertains—viz., when, after being properly educated, people are left to find their places for themselves, do they not spontaneously class themselves in a manner much more conformable to their unequal or dissimilar aptitudes, than governments or social institutions are likely to do it for them? The Sovereignty of the People, again,—that metaphysical axiom which in France and the rest of the Continent has so long been the theoretic basis of radical and democratic politics,—he regards as of a purely negative character, signifying the right of the people to rid themselves by insurrection of a social order that has become oppressive; but, when erected into a positive principle of government, which condemns indefinitely all superiors to "an arbitrary dependence upon the multitude of their inferiors," he considers it as a sort of "transportation to peoples of the divine right so much reproached to kings" (iv. 55, 56). On the doctrine as a metaphysical dogma or an absolute principle, this criticism is just; but there is also a Positive doctrine, without any pretension to being absolute, which claims the direct participation of the governed in their own government, not as a natural right, but as a means to important ends, under the conditions and with the limitations which those ends impose. The general result of M. Comte's criticism on the revolutionary philosophy, is that he deems it not only incapable of aiding the necessary reorganization of society, but a serious impediment thereto, by setting up, on all the great interests of mankind, the mere negation of authority, direction, or organization, as the most perfect state, and the solution of all problems: the extreme point of this aberration being reached by Rousseau and his followers, when they extolled the savage state, as an ideal from which civilization was only a degeneracy, more or less marked and complete.

The state of sociological speculation being such as has been described—divided between a feudal and theological school, now effete, and a democratic and metaphysical one, of no value except for the destruction of the former; the problem, how to render the social science positive, must naturally have presented itself, more or less distinctly, to superior minds. M. Comte examines and criticises, for the most part justly, some of the principal efforts which have been made by individual thinkers for this purpose. But the weak side of his philosophy comes out prominently in his strictures on the only systematic attempt yet made by any body of thinkers, to constitute a science, not indeed of social phenomena generally, but of one great class or division of them. We mean, of course, political economy, which (with a reservation in favour of the speculations of Adam Smith as valuable preparatory studies for science) he deems unscientific, unpositive, and a mere branch of metaphysics, that comprehensive category of condemnation in which he places all attempts at positive science which are not in his opinion directed by a right scientific method. Any one acquainted with the writings of political economists need only read his few pages of animadversions on them (iv. 193 to 205), to learn how extremely superficial M. Comte can sometimes be. He affirms that they have added nothing really new to the original *aperçus* of Adam Smith; when every one who has read them knows that they have added so much as to have changed the whole aspect of the science, besides rectifying and clearing up in the most essential points the *aperçus* themselves. He lays an almost puerile stress, for the purpose of disparagement, on the discussions about the meaning of words which are found in the best books on political economy, as if such discussions were not an indispensable accompaniment of the progress of thought, and abundant in the history of every physical science. On the whole question he has but one remark of any value, and that he misapplies; namely, that the study of the conditions of national wealth as a detached subject is unphilosophical, because, all the different aspects of social phaenomena acting and reacting on one another, they cannot be rightly understood apart: which by no means proves that the material and industrial phaenomena of society are not, even by themselves, susceptible of useful generalizations, but only that these generalizations must necessarily be relative to a given form of civilization and a given stage of social advancement. This, we apprehend, is what no political economist would deny. None of them pretend that the laws of wages, profits, values, prices, and the like, set down in their treatises, would be strictly true, or many of them true at all, in the savage state (for example), or in a community composed of masters and slaves. But they do think, with good reason, that whoever understands the political economy of a country with the complicated and manifold civilization of the nations of Europe, can deduce without difficulty the political economy of any other state of society, with the particular circumstances of which he is equally well acquainted.[14] We do not pretend that political economy has never been prosecuted or taught in a contracted spirit. As often as a study is cultivated by narrow minds, they will draw from it narrow conclusions. If a political economist is deficient in general knowledge, he will exaggerate the importance and universality of the limited class of truths which he knows. All kinds of scientific men are liable to this imputation, and M. Comte is never weary of urging it against them; reproaching them with their narrowness of mind, the petty scale of their thoughts, their incapacity for large views, and the stupidity of those they occasionally attempt beyond the bounds of their own subjects. Political economists do not deserve these reproaches more than other classes of positive inquirers, but less than most. The principal error of narrowness with which they are frequently chargeable, is that of regarding, not any economical doctrine, but their present experience of mankind, as of universal validity; mistaking temporary or local phases of human character for human nature itself; having no faith in the wonderful pliability of the human mind; deeming it impossible, in spite of the strongest evidence, that the earth can produce human beings of a different type from that which is familiar to them in their own age, or even, perhaps, in their own country. The only security against this narrowness is a liberal mental cultivation, and all it proves is that a person is not likely to be a good political economist who is nothing else.

Thus far, we have had to do with M. Comte, as a sociologist, only in his critical capacity. We have now to deal with him as a constructor—the author of a sociological system. The first question is that of the Method proper to the study. His view of this is highly instructive.

The Method proper to the Science of Society must be, in substance, the same as in all other sciences; the interrogation and interpretation of experience, by the twofold process of Induction and Deduction. But its mode of practising these operations has features of peculiarity. In general, Induction furnishes to science the laws of the elementary facts, from which, when known, those of the complex combinations are thought out deductively: specific observation of complex phaenomena yields no general laws, or only empirical ones; its scientific function is to verify the laws obtained by deduction. This mode of philosophizing is not adequate to the exigencies of sociological investigation. In social phaemomena the elementary facts are feelings and actions, and the laws of these are the laws of human nature, social facts being the results of human acts and situations. Since, then, the phaenomena of man in society result from his nature as an individual being, it might be thought that the proper mode of constructing a positive Social Science must be by deducing it from the general laws of human nature, using the facts of history merely for verification. Such, accordingly, has been the conception of social science by many of those who have endeavoured to render it positive, particularly by the school of Bentham. M. Comte considers this as an error. We may, he says, draw from the universal laws of human nature some conclusions (though even these, we think, rather precarious) concerning the very earliest stages of human progress, of which there are either no, or very imperfect, historical records. But as society proceeds in its development, its phaenomena are determined, more and more, not by the simple tendencies of universal human nature, but by the accumulated influence of past generations over the present. The human beings themselves, on the laws of whose nature the facts of history depend, are not abstract or universal but historical human beings, already shaped, and made what they are, by human society. This being the case, no powers of deduction could enable any one, starting from the mere conception of the Being Man, placed in a world such as the earth may have been before the commencement of human agency, to predict and calculate the phaenomena of his development such as they have in fact proved. If the facts of history, empirically considered, had not given rise to any generalizations, a deductive study of history could never have reached higher than more or less plausible conjecture. By good fortune (for the case might easily have been otherwise) the history of our species, looked at as a comprehensive whole, does exhibit a determinate course, a certain order of development: though history alone cannot prove this to be a necessary law, as distinguished from a temporary accident. Here, therefore, begins the office of Biology (or, as we should say, of Psychology) in the social science. The universal laws of human nature are part of the data of sociology, but in using them we must reverse the method of the deductive physical sciences: for while, in these, specific experience commonly serves to verify laws arrived at by deduction, in sociology it is specific experience which suggests the laws, and deduction which verifies them. If a sociological theory, collected from historical evidence, contradicts the established general laws of human nature; if (to use M. Comte's instances) it implies, in the mass of mankind, any very decided natural bent, either in a good or in a bad direction; if it supposes that the reason, in average human beings, predominates over the desires, or the disinterested desires over the personal; we may know that history has been misinterpreted, and that the theory is false. On the other hand, if laws of social phaenomena, empirically generalized from history, can when once suggested be affiliated to the known laws of human nature; if the direction actually taken by the developments and changes of human society, can be seen to be such as the properties of man and of his dwelling-place made antecedently probable, the empirical generalizations are raised into positive laws, and Sociology becomes a science.

Much has been said and written for centuries past, by the practical or empirical school of politicians, in condemnation of theories founded on principles of human nature, without an historical basis; and the theorists, in their turn, have successfully retaliated on the practicalists. But we know not any thinker who, before M. Comte, had penetrated to the philosophy of the matter, and placed the necessity of historical studies as the foundation of sociological speculation on the true footing. From this time any political thinker who fancies himself able to dispense with a connected view of the great facts of history, as a chain of causes and effects, must be regarded as below the level of the age; while the vulgar mode of using history, by looking in it for parallel cases, as if any cases were parallel, or as if a single instance, or even many instances not compared and analysed, could reveal a law, will be more than ever, and irrevocably, discredited.

The inversion of the ordinary relation between Deduction and Induction is not the only point in which, according to M. Comte, the Method proper to Sociology differs from that of the sciences of inorganic nature. The common order of science proceeds from the details to the whole. The method of Sociology should proceed from the whole to the details. There is no universal principle for the order of study, but that of proceeding from the known to the unknown; finding our way to the facts at whatever point is most open to our observation. In the phaenomena of the social state, the collective phaenomenon is more accessible to us than the parts of which it is composed. This is already, in a great degree, true of the mere animal body. It is essential to the idea of an organism, and it is even more true of the social organism than of the individual. The state of every part of the social whole at any time, is intimately connected with the contemporaneous state of all the others. Religious belief, philosophy, science, the fine arts, the industrial arts, commerce, navigation, government, all are in close mutual dependence on one another, insomuch that when any considerable change takes place in one, we may know that a parallel change in all the others has preceded or will follow it. The progress of society from one general state to another is not an aggregate of partial changes, but the product of a single impulse, acting through all the partial agencies, and can therefore be most easily traced by studying them together. Could it even be detected in them separately, its true nature could not be understood except by examining them in the *ensemble*. In constructing, therefore, a theory of society, all the different aspects of the social organization must be taken into consideration at once.

Our space is not consistent with inquiring into all the limitations of this doctrine. It requires many of which M. Comte's theory takes no account. There is one, in particular, dependent on a scientific artifice familiar to students of science, especially of the applications of mathematics to the study of nature. When an effect depends on several variable conditions, some of which change less, or more slowly, than others, we are often able to determine, either by reasoning or by experiment, what would be the law of variation of the effect if its changes depended only on some of the conditions, the remainder being supposed constant. The law so found will be sufficiently near the truth for all times and places in which the latter set of conditions do not vary greatly, and will be a basis to set out from when it becomes necessary to allow for the variations of those conditions also. Most of the conclusions of social science applicable to practical use are of this description. M. Comte's system makes no room for them. We have seen how he deals with the part of them which are the most scientific in character, the generalizations of political economy.

There is one more point in the general philosophy of sociology requiring notice. Social phaenomena, like all others, present two aspects, the statical, and the dynamical; the phaenomena of equilibrium, and those of motion. The statical aspect is that of the laws of social existence, considered abstractedly from progress, and confined to what is common to the progressive and the stationary state. The dynamical aspect is that of social progress. The statics of society is the study of the conditions of existence and permanence of the social state. The dynamics studies the laws of its evolution. The first is the theory of the *consensus,* or interdependence of social phaenomena. The second is the theory of their filiation.

The first division M. Comte, in his great work, treats in a much more summary manner than the second; and it forms, to our thinking, the weakest part of the treatise. He can hardly have seemed even to himself to have originated, in the statics of society, anything new,[15] unless his revival of the Catholic idea of a Spiritual Power may be so considered. The remainder, with the exception of detached thoughts, in which even his feeblest productions are always rich, is trite, while in our judgment far from being always true.

He begins by a statement of the general properties of human nature which make social existence possible. Man has a spontaneous propensity to the society of his fellow-beings, and seeks it instinctively, for its own sake, and not out of regard to the advantages it procures for him, which, in many conditions of humanity, must appear to him very problematical. Man has also a certain, though moderate, amount of natural benevolence. On the other hand, these social propensities are by nature weaker than his selfish ones; and the social state, being mainly kept in existence through the former, involves an habitual antagonism between the two. Further, our wants of all kinds, from the purely organic upwards, can only be satisfied by means of labour, nor does bodily labour suffice, without the guidance of intelligence. But labour, especially when prolonged and monotonous, is naturally hateful, and mental labour the most irksome of all; and hence a second antagonism, which must exist in all societies whatever. The character of the society is principally determined by the degree in which the better incentive, in each of these cases, makes head against the worse. In both the points, human nature is capable of great amelioration. The social instincts may approximate much nearer to the strength of the personal ones, though never entirely coming up to it; the aversion to labour in general, and to intellectual labour in particular, may be much weakened, and the predominance of the inclinations over the reason greatly diminished, though never completely destroyed. The spirit of improvement results from the increasing strength of the social instincts, combined with the growth of an intellectual activity, which guiding the personal propensities, inspires each individual with a deliberate desire to improve his condition. The personal instincts left to their own guidance, and the indolence and apathy natural to mankind, are the sources which mainly feed the spirit of Conservation. The struggle between the two spirits is an universal incident of the social state.

The next of the universal elements in human society is family life; which M. Comte regards as originally the sole, and always the principal, source of the social feelings, and the only school open to mankind in general, in which unselfishness can be learnt, and the feelings and conduct demanded by social relations be made habitual. M. Comte takes this opportunity of declaring his opinions on the proper constitution of the family, and in particular of the marriage institution. They are of the most orthodox and conservative sort. M. Comte adheres not only to the popular Christian, but to the Catholic view of marriage in its utmost strictness, and rebukes Protestant nations for having tampered with the indissolubility of the engagement, by permitting divorce. He admits that the marriage institution has been, in various respects, beneficially modified with the advance of society, and that we may not yet have reached the last of these modifications; but strenuously maintains that such changes cannot possibly affect what he regards as the essential principles of the institution—the irrevocability of the engagement, and the complete subordination of the wife to the husband, and of women generally to men; which are precisely the great vulnerable points of the existing constitution of society on this important subject. It is unpleasant to have to say it of a philosopher, but the incidents of his life which have been made public by his biographers afford an explanation of one of these two opinions: he had quarrelled with his wife.[16] At a later period, under the influence of circumstances equally personal, his opinions and feelings respecting women were very much modified, without becoming more rational: in his final scheme of society, instead of being treated as grown children, they were exalted into goddesses: honours, privileges, and immunities, were lavished on them, only not simple justice. On the other question, the irrevocability of marriage, M. Comte must receive credit for impartiality, since the opposite doctrine would have better suited his personal convenience: but we can give him no other credit, for his argument is not only futile but refutes itself. He says that with liberty of divorce, life would be spent in a constant succession of experiments and failures; and in the same breath congratulates himself on the fact, that modern manners and sentiments have in the main prevented the baneful effects which the toleration of divorce in Protestant countries might have been expected to produce. He did not perceive that if modern habits and feelings have successfully resisted what he deems the tendency of a less rigorous marriage law, it must be because modern habits and feelings are inconsistent with the perpetual series of new trials which he dreaded. If there are tendencies in human nature which seek change and variety, there are others which demand fixity, in matters which touch the daily sources of happiness; and one who had studied history as much as M. Comte, ought to have known that ever since the nomad mode of life was exchanged for the agricultural, the latter tendencies have been always gaining ground on the former. All experience testifies that regularity in domestic relations is almost in direct proportion to industrial civilization. Idle life, and military life with its long intervals of idleness, are the conditions to which, either sexual profligacy, or prolonged vagaries of imagination on that subject, are congenial. Busy men have no time for them, and have too much other occupation for their thoughts: they require that home should be a place of rest, not of incessantly renewed excitement and disturbance. In the condition, therefore, into which modern society has passed, there is no probability that marriages would often be contracted without a sincere desire on both sides that they should be permanent. That this has been the case hitherto in countries where divorce was permitted, we have on M. Comte's own showing: and everything leads us to believe that the power, if granted elsewhere, would in general be used only for its legitimate purpose—for enabling those who, by a blameless or excusable mistake, have lost their first throw for domestic happiness, to free themselves (with due regard for all interests concerned) from the burthensome yoke, and try, under more favourable auspices, another chance. Any further discussion of these great social questions would evidently be incompatible with the nature and limits of the present paper.

Lastly, a phaenomenon universal in all societies, and constantly assuming a wider extension as they advance in their progress, is the co-operation of mankind one with another, by the division of employments and interchange of commodities and services; a communion which extends to nations as well as individuals. The economic importance of this spontaneous organization of mankind as joint workers with and for one another, has often been illustrated. Its moral effects, in connecting them by their interests, and as a more remote consequence, by their sympathies, are equally salutary. But there are some things to be said on the other side. The increasing specialisation of all employments; the division of mankind into innumerable small fractions, each engrossed by an extremely minute fragment of the business of society, is not without inconveniences, as well moral as intellectual, which, if they could not be remedied, would be a serious abatement from the benefits of advanced civilization. The interests of the whole—the bearings of things on the ends of the social union—are less and less present to the minds of men who have so contracted a sphere of activity. The insignificant detail which forms their whole occupation—the infinitely minute wheel they help to turn in the machinery of society—does not arouse or gratify any feeling of public spirit, or unity with their fellow-men. Their work is a mere tribute to physical necessity, not the glad performance of a social office. This lowering effect of the extreme division of labour tells most of all on those who are set up as the lights and teachers of the rest. A man's mind is as fatally narrowed, and his feelings towards the great ends of humanity as miserably stunted, by giving all his thoughts to the classification of a few insects or the resolution of a few equations, as to sharpening the points or putting on the heads of pins. The "dispersive speciality" of the present race of scientific men, who, unlike their predecessors, have a positive aversion to enlarged views, and seldom either know or care for any of the interests of mankind beyond the narrow limits of their pursuit, is dwelt on by M. Comte as one of the great and growing evils of the time, and the one which most retards moral and intellectual regeneration. To contend against it is one of the main purposes towards which he thinks the forces of society should be directed. The obvious remedy is a large and liberal general education, preparatory to all special pursuits: and this is M. Comte's opinion: but the education of youth is not in his estimation enough: he requires an agency set apart for obtruding upon all classes of persons through the whole of life, the paramount claims of the general interest, and the comprehensive ideas that demonstrate the mode in which human actions promote or impair it. In other words, he demands a moral and intellectual authority, charged with the duty of guiding men's opinions and enlightening and warning their consciences; a Spiritual Power, whose judgments on all matters of high moment should deserve, and receive, the same universal respect and deference which is paid to the united judgment of astronomers in matters astronomical. The very idea of such an authority implies that an unanimity has been attained, at least in essentials, among moral and political thinkers, corresponding or approaching to that which already exists in the other sciences. There cannot be this unanimity, until the true methods of positive science have been applied to all subjects, as completely as they have been applied to the study of physical science: to this, however, there is no real obstacle; and when once it is accomplished, the same degree of accordance will naturally follow. The undisputed authority which astronomers possess in astronomy, will be possessed on the great social questions by Positive Philosophers; to whom will belong the spiritual government of society, subject to two conditions: that they be entirely independent, within their own sphere, of the temporal government, and that they be peremptorily excluded from all share in it, receiving instead the entire conduct of education.

This is the leading feature in M. Comte's conception of a regenerated society; and however much this ideal differs from that which is implied more or less confusedly in the negative philosophy of the last three centuries, we hold the amount of truth in the two to be about the same. M. Comte has got hold of half the truth, and the so-called liberal or revolutionary school possesses the other half; each sees what the other does not see, and seeing it exclusively, draws consequences from it which to the other appear mischievously absurd. It is, without doubt, the necessary condition of mankind to receive most of their opinions on the authority of those who have specially studied the matters to which they relate. The wisest can act on no other rule, on subjects with which they are not themselves thoroughly conversant; and the mass of mankind have always done the like on all the great subjects of thought and conduct, acting with implicit confidence on opinions of which they did not know, and were often incapable of understanding, the grounds, but on which as long as their natural guides were unanimous they fully relied, growing uncertain and sceptical only when these became divided, and teachers who as far as they could judge were equally competent, professed contradictory opinions. Any doctrines which come recommended by the nearly universal verdict of instructed minds will no doubt continue to be, as they have hitherto been, accepted without misgiving by the rest. The difference is, that with the wide diffusion of scientific education among the whole people, demanded by M. Comte, their faith, however implicit, would not be that of ignorance: it would not be the blind submission of dunces to men of knowledge, but the intelligent deference of those who know much, to those who know still more. It is those who have some knowledge of astronomy, not those who have none at all, who best appreciate how prodigiously more Lagrange or Laplace knew than themselves. This is what can be said in favour of M. Comte. On the contrary side it is to be said, that in order that this salutary ascendancy over opinion should be exercised by the most eminent thinkers, it is not necessary that they should be associated and organized. The ascendancy will come of itself when the unanimity is attained, without which it is neither desirable nor possible. It is because astronomers agree in their teaching that astronomy is trusted, and not because there is an Academy of Sciences or a Royal Society issuing decrees or passing resolutions. A constituted moral authority can only be required when the object is not merely to promulgate and diffuse principles of conduct, but to direct the detail of their application; to declare and inculcate, not duties, but each person's duty, as was attempted by the spiritual authority of the middle ages. From this extreme application of his principle M. Comte does not shrink. A function of this sort, no doubt, may often be very usefully discharged by individual members of the speculative class; but if entrusted to any organized body, would involve nothing less than a spiritual despotism. This however is what M. Comte really contemplated, though it would practically nullify that peremptory separation of the spiritual from the temporal power, which he justly deemed essential to a wholesome state of society. Those whom an irresistible public opinion invested with the right to dictate or control the acts of rulers, though without the means of backing their advice by force, would have all the real power of the temporal authorities, without their labours or their responsibilities. M. Comte would probably have answered that the temporal rulers, having the whole legal power in their hands, would certainly not pay to the spiritual authority more than a very limited obedience: which amounts to saying that the ideal form of society which he sets up, is only fit to be an ideal because it cannot possibly be realized.

That education should be practically directed by the philosophic class, when there is a philosophic class who have made good their claim to the place in opinion hitherto filled by the clergy, would be natural and indispensable. But that all education should be in the hands of a centralized authority, whether composed of clergy or of philosophers, and be consequently all framed on the same model, and directed to the perpetuation of the same type, is a state of things which instead of becoming more acceptable, will assuredly be more repugnant to mankind, with every step of their progress in the unfettered exercise of their highest faculties. We shall see, in the Second Part, the evils with which the conception of the new Spiritual Power is pregnant, coming out into full bloom in the more complete development which M. Comte gave to the idea in his later years.

After this unsatisfactory attempt to trace the outline of Social Statics, M. Comte passes to a topic on which he is much more at home—the subject of his most eminent speculations; Social Dynamics, or the laws of the evolution of human society.

Two questions meet us at the outset: Is there a natural evolution in human affairs? and is that evolution an improvement? M. Comte resolves them both in the affirmative by the same answer. The natural progress of society consists in the growth of our human attributes, comparatively to our animal and our purely organic ones: the progress of our humanity towards an ascendancy over our animality, ever more nearly approached though incapable of being completely realized. This is the character and tendency of human development, or of what is called civilization; and the obligation of seconding this movement—of working in the direction of it—is the nearest approach which M. Comte makes in this treatise to a general principle or standard of morality.

But as our more eminent, and peculiarly human, faculties are of various orders, moral, intellectual, and aesthetic, the question presents itself, is there any one of these whose development is the predominant agency in the evolution of our species? According to M. Comte, the main agent in the progress of mankind is their intellectual development.

Not because the intellectual is the most powerful part of our nature, for, limited to its inherent strength, it is one of the weakest: but because it is the guiding part, and acts not with its own strength alone, but with the united force of all parts of our nature which it can draw after it. In a social state the feelings and propensities cannot act with their full power, in a determinate direction, unless the speculative intellect places itself at their head. The passions are, in the individual man, a more energetic power than a mere intellectual conviction; but the passions tend to divide, not to unite, mankind: it is only by a common belief that passions are brought to work together, and become a collective force instead of forces neutralizing one another. Our intelligence is first awakened by the stimulus of our animal wants and of our stronger and coarser desires; and these for a long time almost exclusively determine the direction in which our intelligence shall work: but once roused to activity, it assumes more and more the management of the operations of which stronger impulses are the prompters, and constrains them to follow its lead, not by its own strength, but because in the play of antagonistic forces, the path it points out is (in scientific phraseology) the direction of least resistance. Personal interests and feelings, in the social state, can only obtain the maximum of satisfaction by means of co-operation, and the necessary condition of co-operation is a common belief. All human society, consequently, is grounded on a system of fundamental opinions, which only the speculative faculty can provide, and which when provided, directs our other impulses in their mode of seeking their gratification. And hence the history of opinions, and of the speculative faculty, has always been the leading element in the history of mankind.

This doctrine has been combated by Mr Herbert Spencer, in the pamphlet already referred to; and we will quote, in his own words, the theory he propounds in opposition to it:—

"Ideas do not govern and overthrow the world; the world is governed or overthrown by feelings, to which ideas serve only as guides. The social mechanism does not rest finally upon opinions, but almost wholly upon character. Not intellectual anarchy, but moral antagonism, is the cause of political crises. All social phaenomena are produced by the totality of human emotions and beliefs, of which the emotions are mainly predetermined, while the beliefs are mainly post-determined. Men's desires are chiefly inherited; but their beliefs are chiefly acquired, and depend on surrounding conditions; and the most important surrounding conditions depend on the social state which the prevalent desires have produced. The social state at any time existing, is the resultant of all the ambitions, self-interests, fears, reverences, indignations, sympathies, &c., of ancestral citizens and existing citizens. The ideas current in this social state must, on the average, lie congruous with the feelings of citizens, and therefore, on the average, with the social state these feelings have produced. Ideas wholly foreign to this social state cannot be evolved, and if introduced from without, cannot get accepted—or, if accepted, die out when the temporary phase of feeling which caused their acceptance ends. Hence, though advanced ideas, when once established, act upon society and aid its further advance, yet the establishment of such ideas depends on the fitness of society for receiving them. Practically, the popular character and the social state determine what ideas shall be current; instead of the current ideas determining the social state and the character. The modification of men's moral natures, caused by the continuous discipline of social life, which adapts them more and more to social relations, is therefore the chief proximate cause of social progress."[17]

A great part of these statements would have been acknowledged as true by M. Comte, and belong as much to his theory as to Mr Spencer's. The re-action of all other mental and social elements upon the intellectual not only is fully recognized by him, but his philosophy of history makes great use of it, pointing out that the principal intellectual changes could not have taken place unless changes in other elements of society had preceded; but also showing that these were themselves consequences of prior intellectual changes. It will not be found, on a fair examination of what M. Comte has written, that he has overlooked any of the truth that there is in Mr Spencer's theory. He would not indeed have said (what Mr Spencer apparently wishes us to say) that the effects which can be historically traced, for example to religion, were not produced by the belief in God, but by reverence and fear of him. He would have said that the reverence and fear presuppose the belief: that a God must be believed in before he can be feared or reverenced. The whole influence of the belief in a God upon society and civilization, depends on the powerful human sentiments which are ready to attach themselves to the belief; and yet the sentiments are only a social force at all, through the definite direction given to them by that or some other intellectual conviction; nor did the sentiments spontaneously throw up the belief in a God, since in themselves they were equally capable of gathering round some other object. Though it is true that men's passions and interests often dictate their opinions, or rather decide their choice among the two or three forms of opinion, which the existing condition of human intelligence renders possible, this disturbing cause is confined to morals, politics, and religion; and it is the intellectual movement in other regions than these, which is at the root of all the great changes in human affairs. It was not human emotions and passions which discovered the motion of the earth, or detected the evidence of its antiquity; which exploded Scholasticism, and inaugurated the exploration of nature; which invented printing, paper, and the mariner's compass. Yet the Reformation, the English and French revolutions, and still greater moral and social changes yet to come, are direct consequences of these and similar discoveries. Even alchemy and astrology were not believed because people thirsted for gold and were anxious to pry into the future, for these desires are as strong now as they were then: but because alchemy and astrology were conceptions natural to a particular stage in the growth of human knowledge, and consequently determined during that stage the particular means whereby the passions which always exist, sought their gratification. To say that men's intellectual beliefs do not determine their conduct, is like saying that the ship is moved by the steam and not by the steersman. The steam indeed is the motive power; the steersman, left to himself, could not advance the vessel a single inch; yet it is the steersman's will and the steersman's knowledge which decide in what direction it shall move and whither it shall go.

Examining next what is the natural order of intellectual progress among mankind, M. Comte observes, that as their general mode of conceiving the universe must give its character to all their conceptions of detail, the determining fact in their intellectual history must be the natural succession of theories of the universe; which, it has been seen, consists of three stages, the theological, the metaphysical, and the positive. The passage of mankind through these stages, including the successive modifications of the theological conception by the rising influence of the other two, is, to M. Comte's mind, the most decisive fact in the evolution of humanity. Simultaneously, however, there has been going on throughout history a parallel movement in the purely temporal department of things, consisting of the gradual decline of the military mode of life (originally the chief occupation of all freemen) and its replacement by the industrial. M. Comte maintains that there is a necessary connexion and interdependence between this historical sequence and the other: and he easily shows that the progress of industry and that of positive science are correlative; man's power to modify the facts of nature evidently depending on the knowledge he has acquired of their laws. We do not think him equally successful in showing a natural connexion between the theological mode of thought and the military system of society: but since they both belong to the same age of the world—since each is, in itself, natural and inevitable, and they are together modified and together undermined by the same cause, the progress of science and industry, M. Comte is justified in considering them as linked together, and the movement by which mankind emerge from them as a single evolution.

These propositions having been laid down as the first principles of social dynamics, M. Comte proceeds to verify and apply them by a connected view of universal history. This survey nearly fills two large volumes, above a third of the work, in all of which there is scarcely a sentence that does not add an idea. We regard it as by far his greatest achievement, except his review of the sciences, and in some respects more striking even than that. We wish it were practicable in the compass of an essay like the present, to give even a faint conception of the extraordinary merits of this historical analysis. It must be read to be appreciated. Whoever disbelieves that the philosophy of history can be made a science, should suspend his judgment until he has read these volumes of M. Comte. We do not affirm that they would certainly change his opinion; but we would strongly advise him to give them a chance.

We shall not attempt the vain task of abridgment, a few words are all we can give to the subject. M. Comte confines himself to the main stream of human progress, looking only at the races and nations that led the van, and regarding as the successors of a people not their actual descendants, but those who took up the thread of progress after them. His object is to characterize truly, though generally, the successive states of society through which the advanced guard of our species has passed, and the filiation of these states on one another—how each grew out of the preceding and was the parent of the following state. A more detailed explanation, taking into account minute differences and more special and local phaenomena, M. Comte does not aim at, though he does not avoid it when it falls in his path. Here, as in all his other speculations, we meet occasional misjudgments, and his historical correctness in minor matters is now and then at fault; but we may well wonder that it is not oftener so, considering the vastness of the field, and a passage in one of his prefaces in which he says of himself that he *rapidly* amassed the materials for his great enterprise (vi. 34). This expression in his mouth does not imply what it would in that of the majority of men, regard being had to his rare capacity of prolonged and concentrated mental labour: and it is wonderful that he so seldom gives cause to wish that his collection of materials had been less "rapid." But (as he himself remarks) in an inquiry of this sort the vulgarest facts are the most important. A movement common to all mankind—to all of them at least who do move—must depend on causes affecting them all; and these, from the scale on which they operate, cannot require abstruse research to bring them to light: they are not only seen, but best seen, in the most obvious, most universal, and most undisputed phaenomena. Accordingly M. Comte lays no claim to new views respecting the mere facts of history; he takes them as he finds them, builds almost exclusively on those concerning which there is no dispute, and only tries what positive results can be obtained by combining them. Among the vast mass of historical observations which he has grouped and co-ordinated, if we have found any errors they are in things which do not affect his main conclusions. The chain of causation by which he connects the spiritual and temporal life of each era with one another and with the entire series, will be found, we think, in all essentials, irrefragable. When local or temporary disturbing causes have to be taken into the account as modifying the general movement, criticism has more to say. But this will only become important when the attempt is made to write the history or delineate the character of some given society on M. Comte's principles.

Such doubtful statements, or misappreciations of states of society, as we have remarked, are confined to cases which stand more or less apart from the principal line of development of the progressive societies. For instance, he makes greatly too much of what, with many other Continental thinkers, he calls the Theocratic state. He regards this as a natural, and at one time almost an universal, stage of social progress, though admitting that it either never existed or speedily ceased in the two ancient nations to which mankind are chiefly indebted for being permanently progressive. We hold it doubtful if there ever existed what M. Comte means by a theocracy. There was indeed no lack of societies in which, the civil and penal law being supposed to have been divinely revealed, the priests were its authorized interpreters. But this is the case even in Mussulman countries, the extreme opposite of theocracy. By a theocracy we understand to be meant, and we understand M. Comte to mean, a society founded on caste, and in which the speculative, necessarily identical with the priestly caste, has the temporal government in its hands or under its control. We believe that no such state of things ever existed in the societies commonly cited as theocratic. There is no reason to think that in any of them, the king, or chief of the government, was ever, unless by occasional usurpation, a member of the priestly caste.[18] It was not so in Israel, even in the time of the Judges; Jephtha, for example, was a Gileadite, of the tribe of Manasseh, and a military captain, as all governors in such an age and country needed to be. Priestly rulers only present themselves in two anomalous cases, of which next to nothing is known: the Mikados of Japan and the Grand Lamas of Thibet: in neither of which instances was the general constitution of society one of caste, and in the latter of them the priestly sovereignty is as nominal as it has become in the former. India is the typical specimen of the institution of caste—the only case in which we are certain that it ever really existed, for its existence anywhere else is a matter of more or less probable inference in the remote past. But in India, where the importance of the sacerdotal order was greater than in any other recorded state of society, the king not only was not a priest, but, consistently with the religious law, could not be one: he belonged to a different caste. The Brahmins were invested with an exalted character of sanctity, and an enormous amount of civil privileges; the king was enjoined to have a council of Brahmin advisers; but practically he took their advice or disregarded it exactly as he pleased. As is observed by the historian who first threw the light of reason on Hindoo society,[19] the king, though in dignity, to judge by the written code, he seemed vastly inferior to the Brahmins, had always the full power of a despotic monarch: the reason being that he had the command of the army, and the control of the public revenue. There is no case known to authentic history in which either of these belonged to the sacerdotal caste. Even in the cases most favourable to them, the priesthood had no voice in temporal affairs, except the "consultative" voice which M. Comte's theory allows to every spiritual power. His collection of materials must have been unusually "rapid" in this instance, for he regards almost all the societies of antiquity, except the Greek and Roman, as theocratic, even Gaul under the Druids, and Persia under Darius; admitting, however, that in these two countries, when they emerge into the light of history, the theocracy had already been much broken down by military usurpation. By what evidence he could have proved that it ever existed, we confess ourselves unable to divine.

The only other imperfection worth noticing here, which we find in M. Comte's view of history, is that he has a very insufficient understanding of the peculiar phaenomena of English development; though he recognizes, and on the whole correctly estimates, its exceptional character in relation to the general European movement. His failure consists chiefly in want of appreciation of Protestantism; which, like almost all thinkers, even unbelievers, who have lived and thought exclusively in a Catholic atmosphere, he sees and knows only on its negative side, regarding the Reformation as a mere destructive movement, stopped short in too early a stage. He does not seem to be aware that Protestantism has any positive influences, other than the general ones of Christianity; and misses one of the most important facts connected with it, its remarkable efficacy, as contrasted with Catholicism, in cultivating the intelligence and conscience of the individual believer. Protestantism, when not merely professed but actually taken into the mind, makes a demand on the intelligence; the mind is expected to be active, not passive, in the reception of it. The feeling of a direct responsibility of the individual immediately to God, is almost wholly a creation of Protestantism. Even when Protestants were nearly as persecuting as Catholics (quite as much so they never were); even when they held as firmly as Catholics that salvation depended on having the true belief, they still maintained that the belief was not to be accepted from a priest, but to be sought and found by the believer, at his eternal peril if he failed; and that no one could answer to God for him, but that he had to answer for himself. The avoidance of fatal error thus became in a great measure a question of culture; and there was the strongest inducement to every believer, however humble, to seek culture and to profit by it. In those Protestant countries, accordingly, whose Churches were not, as the Church of England always was, principally political institutions—in Scotland, for instance, and the New England States—an amount of education was carried down to the poorest of the people, of which there is no other example; every peasant expounded the Bible to his family (many to their neighbours), and had a mind practised in meditation and discussion on all the points of his religious creed. The food may not have been the most nourishing, but we cannot be blind to the sharpening and strengthening exercise which such great topics gave to the understanding—the discipline in abstraction and reasoning which such mental occupation brought down to the humblest layman, and one of the consequences of which was the privilege long enjoyed by Scotland of supplying the greater part of Europe with professors for its universities, and educated and skilled workmen for its practical arts.

This, however, notwithstanding its importance, is, in a comprehensive view of universal history, only a matter of detail. We find no fundamental errors in M. Comte's general conception of history. He is singularly exempt from most of the twists and exaggerations which we are used to find in almost all thinkers who meddle with speculations of this character. Scarcely any of them is so free (for example) from the opposite errors of ascribing too much or too little influence to accident, and to the qualities of individuals. The vulgar mistake of supposing that the course of history has no tendencies of its own, and that great events usually proceed from small causes, or that kings, or conquerors, or the founders of philosophies and religions, can do with society what they please, no one has more completely avoided or more tellingly exposed. But he is equally free from the error of those who ascribe all to general causes, and imagine that neither casual circumstances, nor governments by their acts, nor individuals of genius by their thoughts, materially accelerate or retard human progress. This is the mistake which pervades the instructive writings of the thinker who in England and in our own times bore the nearest, though a very remote, resemblance to M. Comte —the lamented Mr Buckle; who, had he not been unhappily cut off in an early stage of his labours, and before the complete maturity of his powers, would probably have thrown off an error, the more to be regretted as it gives a colour to the prejudice which regards the doctrine of the invariability of natural laws as identical with fatalism. Mr Buckle also fell into another mistake which M. Comte avoided, that of regarding the intellectual as the only progressive element in man, and the moral as too much the same at all times to affect even the annual average of crime. M. Comte shows, on the contrary, a most acute sense of the causes which elevate or lower the general level of moral excellence; and deems intellectual progress in no other way so beneficial as by creating a standard to guide the moral sentiments of mankind, and a mode of bringing those sentiments effectively to bear on conduct.

M. Comte is equally free from the error of considering any practical rule or doctrine that can be laid down in politics as universal and absolute. All political truth he deems strictly relative, implying as its correlative a given state or situation of society. This conviction is now common to him with all thinkers who are on a level with the age, and comes so naturally to any intelligent reader of history, that the only wonder is how men could have been prevented from reaching it sooner. It marks one of the principal differences between the political philosophy of the present time and that of the past; but

M. Comte adopted it when the opposite mode of thinking was still general, and there are few thinkers to whom the principle owes more in the way of comment and illustration.

Again, while he sets forth the historical succession of systems of belief and forms of political society, and places in the strongest light those imperfections in each which make it impossible that any of them should be final, this does not make him for a moment unjust to the men or the opinions of the past. He accords with generous recognition the gratitude due to all who, with whatever imperfections of doctrine or even of conduct, contributed materially to the work of human improvement. In all past modes of thought and forms of society he acknowledged a useful, in many a necessary, office, in carrying mankind through one stage of improvement into a higher. The theological spirit in its successive forms, the metaphysical in its principal varieties, are honoured by him for the services they rendered in bringing mankind out of pristine savagery into a state in which more advanced modes of belief became possible. His list of heroes and benefactors of mankind includes, not only every important name in the scientific movement, from Thales of Miletus to Fourier the mathematician and Blainville the biologist, and in the aesthetic from Homer to Manzoni, but the most illustrious names in the annals of the various religions and philosophies, and the really great politicians in all states of society.[20] Above all, he has the most profound admiration for the services rendered by Christianity, and by the Church of the middle ages. His estimate of the Catholic period is such as the majority of Englishmen (from whom we take the liberty to differ) would deem exaggerated, if not absurd. The great men of Christianity, from St Paul to St Francis of Assisi, receive his warmest homage: nor does he forget the greatness even of those who lived and thought in the centuries in which the Catholic Church, having stopt short while the world had gone on, had become a hindrance to progress instead of a promoter of it; such men as Fénélon and St Vincent de Paul, Bossuet and Joseph de Maistre. A more comprehensive, and, in the primitive sense of the term, more catholic, sympathy and reverence towards real worth, and every kind of service to humanity, we have not met with in any thinker. Men who would have torn each other in pieces, who even tried to do so, if each usefully served in his own way the interests of mankind, are all hallowed to him.

Neither is his a cramped and contracted notion of human excellence, which cares only for certain forms of development. He not only personally appreciates, but rates high in moral value, the creations of poets and artists in all departments, deeming them, by their mixed appeal to the sentiments and the understanding, admirably fitted to educate the feelings of abstract thinkers, and enlarge the intellectual horizon of people of the world.[21] He regards the law of progress as applicable, in spite of appearances, to poetry and art as much as to science and politics. The common impression to the contrary he ascribes solely to the fact, that the perfection of aesthetic creation requires as its condition a consentaneousness in the feelings of mankind, which depends for its existence on a fixed and settled state of opinions: while the last five centuries have been a period not of settling, but of unsettling and decomposing, the most general beliefs and sentiments of mankind. The numerous monuments of poetic and artistic genius which the modern mind has produced even under this great disadvantage, are (he maintains) sufficient proof what great productions it will be capable of, when one harmonious vein of sentiment shall once more thrill through the whole of society, as in the days of Homer, of Aeschylus, of Phidias, and even of Dante.

After so profound and comprehensive a view of the progress of human society in the past, of which the future can only be a prolongation, it is natural to ask, to what use does he put this survey as a basis of practical recommendations? Such recommendations he certainly makes, though, in the present Treatise, they are of a much less definite character than in his later writings. But we miss a necessary link; there is a break in the otherwise close concatenation of his speculations. We fail to see any scientific connexion between his theoretical explanation of the past progress of society, and his proposals for future improvement. The proposals are not, as we might expect, recommended as that towards which human society has been tending and working through the whole of history. It is thus that thinkers have usually proceeded, who formed theories for the future, grounded on historical analysis of the past. Tocqueville, for example, and others, finding, as they thought, through all history, a steady progress in the direction of social and political equality, argued that to smooth this transition, and make the best of what is certainly coming, is the proper employment of political foresight. We do not find M. Comte supporting his recommendations by a similar line of argument. They rest as completely, each on its separate reasons of supposed utility, as with philosophers who, like Bentham, theorize on politics without any historical basis at all. The only bridge of connexion which leads from his historical speculations to his practical conclusions, is the inference, that since the old powers of society, both in the region of thought and of action, are declining and destined to disappear, leaving only the two rising powers, positive thinkers on the one hand, leaders of industry on the other, the future necessarily belongs to these: spiritual power to the former, temporal to the latter. As a specimen of historical forecast this is very deficient; for are there not the masses as well as the leaders of industry? and is not theirs also a growing power? Be this as it may, M. Comte's conceptions of the mode in which these growing powers should be organized and used, are grounded on anything rather than on history. And we cannot but remark a singular anomaly in a thinker of M. Comte's calibre. After the ample evidence he has brought forward of the slow growth of the sciences, all of which except the mathematico-astronomical couple are still, as he justly thinks, in a very early stage, it yet appears as if, to his mind, the mere institution of a positive science of sociology were tantamount to its completion; as if all the diversities of opinion on the subject, which set mankind at variance, were solely owing to its having been studied in the theological or the metaphysical manner, and as if when the positive method which has raised up real sciences on other subjects of knowledge, is similarly employed on this, divergence would at once cease, and the entire body of positive social inquirers would exhibit as much agreement in their doctrines as those who cultivate any of the sciences of inorganic life. Happy would be the prospects of mankind if this were so. A time such as M. Comte reckoned upon may come; unless something stops the progress of human improvement, it is sure to come: but after an unknown duration of hard thought and violent controversy. The period of decomposition, which has lasted, on his own computation, from the beginning of the fourteenth century to the present, is not yet terminated: the shell of the old edifice will remain standing until there is another ready to replace it; and the new synthesis is barely begun, nor is even the preparatory analysis completely finished. On other occasions M. Comte is very well aware that the Method of a science is not the science itself, and that when the difficulty of discovering the right processes has been overcome, there remains a still greater difficulty, that of applying them. This, which is true of all sciences, is truest of all in Sociology. The facts being more complicated, and depending on a greater concurrence of forces, than in any other science, the difficulty of treating them deductively is proportionally increased, while the wide difference between any one case and every other in some of the circumstances which affect the result, makes the pretence of direct induction usually no better than empiricism. It is therefore, out of all proportion, more uncertain than in any other science, whether two inquirers equally competent and equally disinterested will take the same view of the evidence, or arrive at the same conclusion. When to this intrinsic difficulty is added the infinitely greater extent to which personal or class interests and predilections interfere with impartial judgment, the hope of such accordance of opinion among sociological inquirers as would obtain, in mere deference to their authority, the universal assent which M. Comte's scheme of society requires, must be adjourned to an indefinite distance.

M. Comte's own theory is an apt illustration of these difficulties, since, though prepared for these speculations as no one had ever been prepared before, his views of social regeneration even in the rudimentary form in which they appear above-ground in this treatise (not to speak of the singular system into which he afterwards enlarged them) are such as perhaps no other person of equal knowledge and capacity would agree in. Were those views as true as they are questionable, they could not take effect until the unanimity among positive thinkers, to which he looked forward, shall have been attained; since the mainspring of his system is a Spiritual Power composed of positive philosophers, which only the previous attainment of the unanimity in question could call into existence. A few words will sufficiently express the outline of his scheme. A corporation of philosophers, receiving a modest support from the state, surrounded by reverence, but peremptorily excluded not only from all political power or employment, but from all riches, and all occupations except their own, are to have the entire direction of education: together with, not only the right and duty of advising and reproving all persons respecting both their public and their private life, but also a control (whether authoritative or only moral is not defined) over the speculative class itself, to prevent them from wasting time and ingenuity on inquiries and speculations of no value to mankind (among which he includes many now in high estimation), and compel them to employ all their powers on the investigations which may be judged, at the time, to be the most urgently important to the general welfare. The temporal government which is to coexist with this spiritual authority, consists of an aristocracy of capitalists, whose dignity and authority are to be in the ratio of the degree of generality of their conceptions and operations—bankers at the summit, merchants next, then manufacturers, and agriculturists at the bottom of the scale. No representative system, or other popular organization, by way of counterpoise to this governing power, is ever contemplated. The checks relied upon for preventing its abuse, are the counsels and remonstrances of the Spiritual Power, and unlimited liberty of discussion and comment by all classes of inferiors. Of the mode in which either set of authorities should fulfil the office assigned to it, little is said in this treatise: but the general idea is, while regulating as little as possible by law, to make the pressure of opinion, directed by the Spiritual Power, so heavy on every individual, from the humblest to the most powerful, as to render legal obligation, in as many cases as possible, needless. Liberty and spontaneity on the part of individuals form no part of the scheme. M. Comte looks on them with as great jealousy as any scholastic pedagogue, or ecclesiastical director of consciences. Every particular of conduct, public or private, is to be open to the public eye, and to be kept, by the power of opinion, in the course which the Spiritual corporation shall judge to be the most right.

    This is not a sufficiently tempting picture to have much chance of making converts rapidly, and the objections to the scheme are too obvious to need stating. Indeed, it is only thoughtful persons to whom it will be credible, that speculations leading to this result can deserve the attention necessary for understanding them. We propose in the next Essay to examine them as part of the elaborate and coherent system of doctrine, which M. Comte afterwards put together for the reconstruction of society. Meanwhile the reader will gather, from what has been said, that M. Comte has not, in our opinion, created Sociology. Except his analysis of history, to which there is much to be added, but which we do not think likely to be ever, in its general features, superseded, he has done nothing in Sociology which does not require to be done over again, and better. Nevertheless, he has greatly advanced the study. Besides the great stores of thought, of various and often of eminent merit, with which he has enriched the subject, his conception of its method is so much truer and more profound than that of any one who preceded him, as to constitute an era in its cultivation. If it cannot be said of him that he has created a science, it may be said truly that he has, for the first time, made the creation possible. This is a great achievement, and, with the extraordinary merit of his historical analysis, and of his philosophy of the physical sciences, is enough to immortalize his name. But his renown with posterity would probably have been greater than it is now likely to be, if after showing the way in which the social science should be formed, he had not flattered himself that he had formed it, and that it was already sufficiently solid for attempting to build upon its foundation the entire fabric of the Political Art.

PART II.
THE LATER SPECULATIONS OF M. COMTE.[22]

The appended list of publications contain the materials for knowing and estimating what M. Comte termed his second career, in which the *savant*, historian, and philosopher of his fundamental treatise, came forth transfigured as the High Priest of the Religion of Humanity. They include all his writings except the Cours de Philosophic Positive: for his early productions, and the occasional publications of his later life, are reprinted as Preludes or Appendices to the treatises here enumerated, or in Dr Robinet's volume, which, as well as that of M. Littré, also contains copious extracts from his correspondence.

In the concluding pages of his great systematic work, M. Comte had announced four other treatises as in contemplation: on Politics; on the Philosophy of Mathematics; on Education, a project subsequently enlarged to include the systematization of Morals; and on Industry, or the action of man upon external nature. Our list comprises the only two of these which he lived to execute. It further contains a brief exposition of his final doctrines, in the form of a Dialogue, or, as he terms it, a Catechism, of which a translation has been published by his principal English adherent, Mr Congreve. There has also appeared very recently, under the title of "A General View of Positivism," a translation by Dr Bridges, of the Preliminary Discourse in six chapters, prefixed to the Système de Politique Positive. The remaining three books on our list are the productions of disciples in different degrees. M.

Littré, the only thinker of established reputation who accepts that character, is a disciple only of the Cours de Philosophie Positive, and can see the weak points even in that. Some of them he has discriminated and discussed with great judgment: and the merits of his volume, both as a sketch of M. Comte's life and an appreciation of his doctrines, would well deserve a fuller notice than we are able to give it here. M. de Blignières is a far more thorough adherent; so much so, that the reader of his singularly well and attractively written condensation and popularization of his master's doctrines, does not easily discover in what it falls short of that unqualified acceptance which alone, it would seem, could find favour with M. Comte. For he ended by casting off M. de Blignières, as he had previously cast off M. Littré, and every other person who, having gone with him a certain length, refused to follow him to the end. The author of the last work in our enumeration, Dr Robinet, is a disciple after M. Comte's own heart; one whom no difficulty stops, and no absurdity startles. But it is far from our disposition to speak otherwise than respectfully of Dr Robinet and the other earnest men, who maintain round the tomb of their master an organized co-operation for the diffusion of doctrines which they believe destined to regenerate the human race. Their enthusiastic veneration for him, and devotion to the ends he pursued, do honour alike to them and to their teacher, and are an evidence of the personal ascendancy he exercised over those who approached him; an ascendancy which for a time carried away even M. Littré, as he confesses, to a length which his calmer judgment does not now approve.

These various writings raise many points of interest regarding M. Comte's personal history, and some, not without philosophic bearings, respecting his mental habits: from all which matters we shall abstain, with the exception of two, which he himself proclaimed with great emphasis, and a knowledge of which is almost indispensable to an apprehension of the characteristic difference between his second career and his first. It should be known that during his later life, and even before completing his first great treatise, M. Comte adopted a rule, to which he very rarely made any exception: to abstain systematically, not only from newspapers or periodical publications, even scientific, but from all reading whatever, except a few favourite poets in the ancient and modern European languages. This abstinence he practised for the sake of mental health; by way, as he said, of "*hygiène cérébrale.*" We are far from thinking that the practice has nothing whatever to recommend it. For most thinkers, doubtless, it would be a very unwise one; but we will not affirm that it may not sometimes be advantageous to a mind of the peculiar quality of M. Comte's—one that can usefully devote itself to following out to the remotest developments a particular line of meditations, of so arduous a kind that the complete concentration of the intellect upon its own thoughts is almost a necessary condition of success. When a mind of this character has laboriously and conscientiously laid in beforehand, as M. Comte had done, an ample stock of materials, he may be justified in thinking that he will contribute most to the mental wealth of mankind by occupying himself solely in working upon these, without distracting his attention by continually taking in more matter, or keeping a communication open with other independent intellects. The practice, therefore, may be legitimate; but no one should adopt it without being aware of what he loses by it. He must resign the pretension of arriving at the whole truth on the subject, whatever it be, of his meditations. That he should effect this, even on a narrow subject, by the mere force of his own mind, building on the foundations of his predecessors, without aid or correction from his contemporaries, is simply impossible. He may do eminent service by elaborating certain sides of the truth, but he must expect to find that there are other sides which have wholly escaped his attention. However great his powers, everything that he can do without the aid of incessant reminders from other thinkers, is merely provisional, and will require a thorough revision. He ought to be aware of this, and accept it with his eyes open, regarding himself as a pioneer, not a constructor. If he thinks that he can contribute most towards the elements of the final synthesis by following out his own original thoughts as far as they will go, leaving to other thinkers, or to himself at a subsequent time, the business of adjusting them to the thoughts by which they ought to be accompanied, he is right in doing so. But he deludes himself if he imagines that any conclusions he can arrive at, while he practises M. Comte's rule of *hygiène cérébrale*, can possibly be definitive.

Neither is such a practice, in a hygienic point of view, free from the gravest dangers to the philosopher's own mind. When once he has persuaded himself that he can work out the final truth on any subject, exclusively from his own sources, he is apt to lose all measure or standard by which to be apprized when he is departing from common sense. Living only with his own thoughts, he gradually forgets the aspect they present to minds of a different mould from his own; he looks at his conclusions only from the point of view which suggested them, and from which they naturally appear perfect; and every consideration which from other points of view might present itself, either as an objection or as a necessary modification, is to him as if it did not exist. When his merits come to be recognised and appreciated, and especially if he obtains disciples, the intellectual infirmity soon becomes complicated with a moral one. The natural result of the position is a gigantic self-confidence, not to say self-conceit. That of M. Comte is colossal. Except here and there in an entirely self-taught thinker, who has no high standard with which to compare himself, we have met with nothing approaching to it. As his thoughts grew more extravagant, his self-confidence grew more outrageous. The height it ultimately attained must be seen, in his writings, to be believed.

The other circumstance of a personal nature which it is impossible not to notice, because M. Comte is perpetually referring to it as the origin of the great superiority which he ascribes to his later as compared with his earlier speculations, is the "moral regeneration" which he underwent from "une angélique influence" and "une incomparable passion privée." He formed a passionate attachment to a lady whom he describes as uniting everything which is morally with much that is intellectually admirable, and his relation to whom, besides the direct influence of her character upon his own, gave him an insight into the true sources of human happiness, which changed his whole conception of life. This attachment, which always remained pure, gave him but one year of passionate enjoyment, the lady having been cut off by death at the end of that short period; but the adoration of her memory survived, and became, as we shall see, the type of his conception of the sympathetic culture proper for all human beings. The change thus effected in his personal character and sentiments, manifested itself at once in his speculations; which, from having been only a philosophy, now aspired to become a religion; and from having been as purely, and almost rudely, scientific and intellectual, as was compatible with a character always enthusiastic in its admirations and in its ardour for improvement, became from this time what, for want of a better name, may be called sentimental; but sentimental in a way of its own, very curious to contemplate. In considering the system of religion, politics, and morals, which in his later writings M. Comte constructed, it is not unimportant to bear in mind the nature of the personal experience and inspiration to which he himself constantly attributed this phasis of his philosophy. But as we shall have much more to say against, than in favour of, the conclusions to which he was in this manner conducted, it is right to declare that, from the evidence of his writings, we really believe the moral influence of Madame Clotilde de Vaux upon his character to have been of the ennobling as well as softening character which he ascribes to it. Making allowance for the effects of his exuberant growth in self-conceit, we perceive almost as much improvement in his feelings, as deterioration in his speculations, compared with those of the Philosophie Positive. Even the speculations are, in some secondary aspects, improved through the beneficial effect of the improved feelings; and might have been more so, if, by a rare good fortune, the object of his attachment had been qualified to exercise as improving an influence over him intellectually as morally, and if he could have been contented with something less ambitious than being the supreme moral legislator and religious pontiff of the human race.

When we say that M. Comte has erected his philosophy into a religion, the word religion must not be understood in its ordinary sense. He made no change in the purely negative attitude which he maintained towards theology: his religion is without a God. In saying this, we have done enough to induce nine-tenths of all readers, at least in our own country, to avert their faces and close their ears. To have no religion, though scandalous enough, is an idea they are partly used to: but to have no God, and to talk of religion, is to their feelings at once an absurdity and an impiety. Of the remaining tenth, a great proportion, perhaps, will turn away from anything which calls itself by the name of religion at all. Between the two, it is difficult to find an audience who can be induced to listen to M. Comte without an insurmountable prejudice. But, to be just to any opinion, it ought to be considered, not exclusively from an opponent's point of view, but from that of the mind which propounds it. Though conscious of being in an extremely small minority, we venture to think that a religion may exist without belief in a God, and that a religion without a God may be, even to Christians, an instructive and profitable object of contemplation.

What, in truth, are the conditions necessary to constitute a religion? There must be a creed, or conviction, claiming authority over the whole of human life; a belief, or set of beliefs, deliberately adopted, respecting human destiny and duty, to which the believer inwardly acknowledges that all his actions ought to be subordinate. Moreover, there must be a sentiment connected with this creed, or capable of being invoked by it, sufficiently powerful to give it in fact, the authority over human conduct to which it lays claim in theory. It is a great advantage (though not absolutely indispensable) that this sentiment should crystallize, as it were, round a concrete object; if possible a really existing one, though, in all the more important cases, only ideally present. Such an object Theism and Christianity offer to the believer: but the condition may be fulfilled, if not in a manner strictly equivalent, by another object. It has been said that whoever believes in "the Infinite nature of Duty," even if he believe in nothing else, is religious. M. Comte believes in what is meant by the infinite nature of duty, but ho refers the obligations of duty, as well as all sentiments of devotion, to a concrete object, at once ideal and real; the Human Race, conceived as a continuous whole, including the past, the present, and the future. This great collective existence, this "Grand Etre," as he terms it, though the feelings it can excite are necessarily very different from those which direct themselves towards an ideally perfect Being, has, as he forcibly urges, this advantage in respect to us, that it really needs our services, which Omnipotence cannot, in any genuine sense of the term, be supposed to do: and M. Comte says, that assuming the existence of a Supreme Providence (which he is as far from denying as from affirming), the best, and even the only, way in which we can rightly worship or serve Him, is by doing our utmost to love and serve that other Great Being, whose inferior Providence has bestowed on us all the benefits that we owe to the labours and virtues of former generations. It may not be consonant to usage to call this a religion; but the term so applied has a meaning, and one which is not adequately expressed by any other word. Candid persons of all creeds may be willing to admit, that if a person has an ideal object, his attachment and sense of duty towards which are able to control and discipline all his other sentiments and propensities, and prescribe to him a rule of life, that person has a religion: and though everyone naturally prefers his own religion to any other, all must admit that if the object of this attachment, and of this feeling of duty, is the aggregate of our fellow-creatures, this Religion of the Infidel cannot, in honesty and conscience, be called an intrinsically bad one. Many, indeed, may be unable to believe that this object is capable of gathering round it feelings sufficiently strong: but this is exactly the point on which a doubt can hardly remain in an intelligent reader of M. Comte: and we join with him in contemning, as equally irrational and mean, the conception of human nature as incapable of giving its love and devoting its existence to any object which cannot afford in exchange an eternity of personal enjoyment.

The power which may be acquired over the mind by the idea of the general interest of the human race, both as a source of emotion and as a motive to conduct, many have perceived; but we know not if any one, before M. Comte, realized so fully as he has done, all the majesty of which that idea is susceptible. It ascends into the unknown recesses of the past, embraces the manifold present, and descends into the indefinite and unforeseeable future, forming a collective Existence without assignable beginning or end, it appeals to that feeling of the Infinite, which is deeply rooted in human nature, and which seems necessary to the imposingness of all our highest conceptions. Of the vast unrolling web of human life, the part best known to us is irrevocably past; this we can no longer serve, but can still love: it comprises for most of us the far greater number of those who have loved us, or from whom we have received benefits, as well as the long series of those who, by their labours and sacrifices for mankind, have deserved to be held in everlasting and grateful remembrance. As M. Comte truly says, the highest minds, even now, live in thought with the great dead, far more than with the living; and, next to the dead, with those ideal human beings yet to come, whom they are never destined to see. If we honour as we ought those who have served mankind in the past, we shall feel that we are also working for those benefactors by serving that to which their lives were devoted. And when reflection, guided by history, has taught us the intimacy of the connexion of every age of humanity with every other, making us see in the earthly destiny of mankind the playing out of a great drama, or the action of a prolonged epic, all the generations of mankind become indissolubly united into a single image, combining all the power over the mind of the idea of Posterity, with our best feelings towards the living world which surrounds us, and towards the predecessors who have made us what we are. That the ennobling power of this grand conception may have its full efficacy, we should, with M. Comte, regard the Grand Etre, Humanity, or Mankind, as composed, in the past, solely of those who, in every age and variety of position, have played their part worthily in life. It is only as thus restricted that the aggregate of our species becomes an object deserving our veneration. The unworthy members of it are best dismissed from our habitual thoughts; and the imperfections which adhered through life, even to those of the dead who deserve honourable remembrance, should be no further borne in mind than is necessary not to falsify our conception of facts. On the other hand, the Grand Etre in its completeness ought to include not only all whom we venerate, but all sentient beings to which we owe duties, and which have a claim on our attachment. M. Comte, therefore, incorporates into the ideal object whose service is to be the law of our life, not our own species exclusively, but, in a subordinate degree, our humble auxiliaries, those animal races which enter into real society with man, which attach themselves to him, and voluntarily co-operate with him, like the noble dog who gives his life for his human friend and benefactor. For this M. Comte has been subjected to unworthy ridicule, but there is nothing truer or more honourable to him in the whole body of his doctrines. The strong sense he always shows of the worth of the inferior animals, and of the duties of mankind towards them, is one of the very finest traits of his character.

We, therefore, not only hold that M. Comte was justified in the attempt to develope his philosophy into a religion, and had realized the essential conditions of one, but that all other religions are made better in proportion as, in their practical result, they are brought to coincide with that which he aimed at constructing. But, unhappily, the next thing we are obliged to do, is to charge him with making a complete mistake at the very outset of his operations—with fundamentally misconceiving the proper office of a rule of life. He committed the error which is often, but falsely, charged against the whole class of utilitarian moralists; he required that the test of conduct should also be the exclusive motive to it. Because the good of the human race is the ultimate standard of right and wrong, and because moral discipline consists in cultivating the utmost possible repugnance to all conduct injurious to the general good, M. Comte infers that the good of others is the only inducement on which we should allow ourselves to act; and that we should endeavour to starve the whole of the desires which point to our personal satisfaction, by denying them all gratification not strictly required by physical necessities. The golden rule of morality, in M. Comte's religion, is to live for others, "vivre pour autrui." To do as we would be done by, and to love our neighbour as ourself, are not sufficient for him: they partake, he thinks, of the nature of personal calculations. We should endeavour not to love ourselves at all. We shall not succeed in it, but we should make the nearest approach to it possible. Nothing less will satisfy him, as towards humanity, than the sentiment which one of his favourite writers, Thomas à Kempis, addresses to

God: Amem te plus quam me, nec me nisi propter te. All education and all moral discipline should have but one object, to make altruism (a word of his own coming) predominate over egoism. If by this were only meant that egoism is bound, and should be taught, always to give way to the well-understood interests of enlarged altruism, no one who acknowledges any morality at all would object to the proposition. But M. Comte, taking his stand on the biological fact that organs are strengthened by exercise and atrophied by disuse, and firmly convinced that each of our elementary inclinations has its distinct cerebral organ, thinks it the grand duty of life not only to strengthen the social affections by constant habit and by referring all our actions to them, but, as far as possible, to deaden the personal passions and propensities by desuetude. Even the exercise of the intellect is required to obey as an authoritative rule the dominion of the social feelings over the intelligence (du coeur sur l'esprit). The physical and other personal instincts are to be mortified far beyond the demands of bodily health, which indeed the morality of the future is not to insist much upon, for fear of encouraging "les calculs personnels." M. Comte condemns only such austerities as, by diminishing the vigour of the constitution, make us less capable of being useful to others. Any indulgence, even in food, not necessary to health and strength, he condemns as immoral. All gratifications except those of the affections, are to be tolerated only as "inevitable infirmities." Novalis said of Spinoza that he was a God-intoxicated man: M. Comte is a morality-intoxicated man. Every question with him is one of morality, and no motive but that of morality is permitted.

The explanation of this we find in an original mental twist, very common in French thinkers, and by which M. Comte was distinguished beyond them all. He could not dispense with what he called "unity." It was for the sake of Unity that a religion was, in his eyes, desirable. Not in the mere sense of Unanimity, but in a far wider one. A religion must be something by which to "systematize" human life. His definition of it, in the "Catéchisme," is "the state of complete unity which distinguishes our existence, at once personal and social, when all its parts, both moral and physical, converge habitually to a common destination.... Such a harmony, individual and collective, being incapable of complete realization in an existence so complicated as ours, this definition of religion characterizes the immovable type towards which tends more and more the aggregate of human efforts. Our happiness and our merit consist especially in approaching as near as possible to this unity, of which the gradual increase constitutes the best measure of real improvement, personal or social." To this theme he continually returns, and argues that this unity or harmony among all the elements of our life is not consistent with the predominance of the personal propensities, since these drag us in different directions; it can only result from the subordination of them all to the social icelings, which may be made to act in a uniform direction by a common system of convictions, and which differ from the personal inclinations in this, that we all naturally encourage them in one another, while, on the contrary, social life is a perpetual restraint upon the selfish propensities.

The *fons errorum* in M. Comte's later speculations is this inordinate demand for "unity" and "systematization." This is the reason why it does not suffice to him that all should be ready, in case of need, to postpone their personal interests and inclinations to the requirements of the general good: he demands that each should regard as vicious any care at all for his personal interests, except as a means to the good of others—should be ashamed of it, should strive to cure himself of it, because his existence is not "systematized," is not in "complete unity," as long as he cares for more than one thing. The strangest part of the matter is, that this doctrine seems to M. Comte to be axiomatic. That all perfection consists in unity, he apparently considers to be a maxim which no sane man thinks of questioning. It never seems to enter into his conceptions that any one could object *ab initio*, and ask, why this universal systematizing, systematizing, systematizing? Why is it necessary that all human life should point but to one object, and be cultivated into a system of means to a single end? May it not be the fact that mankind, who after all are made up of single human beings, obtain a greater sum of happiness when each pursues his own, under the rules and conditions required by the good of the rest, than when each makes the good of the rest his only subject, and allows himself no personal pleasures not indispensable to the preservation of his faculties? The regimen of a blockaded town should be cheerfully submitted to when high purposes require it, but is it the ideal perfection of human existence? M. Comte sees none of these difficulties. The only true happiness, he affirms, is in the exercise of the affections. He had found it so for a whole year, which was enough to enable him to get to the bottom of the question, and to judge whether he could do without everything else. Of course the supposition was not to be heard of that any other person could require, or be the better for, what M. Comte did not value. "Unity" and "systematization" absolutely demanded that all other people should model themselves after M. Comte. It would never do to suppose that there could be more than one road to human happiness, or more than one ingredient in it.

The most prejudiced must admit that this religion without theology is not chargeable with relaxation of moral restraints. On the contrary, it prodigiously exaggerates them. It makes the same ethical mistake as the theory of Calvinism, that every act in life should be done for the glory of God, and that whatever is not a duty is a sin. It does not perceive that between the region of duty and that of sin there is an intermediate space, the region of positive worthiness. It is not good that persons should be bound, by other people's opinion, to do everything that they would deserve praise for doing. There is a standard of altruism to which all should be required to come up, and a degree beyond it which is not obligatory, but meritorious. It is incumbent on every one to restrain the pursuit of his personal objects within the limits consistent with the essential interests of others. What those limits are, it is the province of ethical science to determine; and to keep all individuals and aggregations of individuals within them, is the proper office of punishment and of moral blame. If in addition to fulfilling this obligation, persons make the good of others a direct object of disinterested exertions, postponing or sacrificing to it even innocent personal indulgences, they deserve gratitude and honour, and are fit objects of moral praise. So long as they are in no way compelled to this conduct by any external pressure, there cannot be too much of it; but a necessary condition is its spontaneity; since the notion of a happiness for all, procured by the self-sacrifice of each, if the abnegation is really felt to be a sacrifice, is a contradiction. Such spontaneity by no means excludes sympathetic encouragement; but the encouragement should take the form of making self-devotion pleasant, not that of making everything else painful. The object should be to stimulate services to humanity by their natural rewards; not to render the pursuit of our own good in any other manner impossible, by visiting it with the reproaches of other and of our own conscience. The proper office of those sanctions is to enforce upon every one, the conduct necessary to give all other persons their fair chance: conduct which chiefly consists in not doing them harm, and not impeding them in anything which without harming others does good to themselves. To this must of course be added, that when we either expressly or tacitly undertake to do more, we are bound to keep our promise. And inasmuch as every one, who avails himself of the advantages of society, leads others to expect from him all such positive good offices and disinterested services as the moral improvement attained by mankind has rendered customary, he deserves moral blame if, without just cause, he disappoints that expectation. Through this principle the domain of moral duty is always widening. When what once was uncommon virtue becomes common virtue, it comes to be numbered among obligations, while a degree exceeding what has grown common, remains simply meritorious.

M. Comte is accustomed to draw most of his ideas of moral cultivation from the discipline of the Catholic Church. Had he followed that guidance in the present case, he would have been less wide of the mark. For the distinction which we have drawn was fully recognized by the sagacious and far-sighted men who created the Catholic ethics. It is even one of the stock reproaches against Catholicism, that it has two standards of morality, and does not make obligatory on all Christians the highest rule of Christian perfection. It has one standard which, faithfully acted up to, suffices for salvation, another and a higher which when realized constitutes a saint. M. Comte, perhaps unconsciously, for there is nothing that he would have been more unlikely to do if he had been aware of it, has taken a leaf out of the book of the despised Protestantism. Like the extreme Calvinists, he requires that all believers shall be saints, and damns then (after his own fashion) if they are not.

Our conception of human life is different. We do not conceive life to be so rich in enjoyments, that it can afford to forego the cultivation of all those which address themselves to what M. Comte terms the egoistic propensities. On the contrary, we believe that a sufficient gratification of these, short of excess, but up to the measure which renders the enjoyment greatest, is almost always favourable to the benevolent affections. The moralization of the personal enjoyments we deem to consist, not in reducing them to the smallest possible amount, but in cultivating the habitual wish to share them with others, and with all others, and scorning to desire anything for oneself which is incapable of being so shared. There is only one passion or inclination which is permanently incompatible with this condition—the love of domination, or superiority, for its own sake; which implies, and is grounded on, the equivalent depression of other people. As a rule of conduct, to be enforced by moral sanctions, we think no more should be attempted than to prevent people from doing harm to others, or omitting to do such good as they have undertaken. Demanding no more than this, society, in any tolerable circumstances, obtains much more; for the natural activity of human nature, shut out from all noxious directions, will expand itself in useful ones. This is our conception of the moral rule prescribed by the religion of Humanity. But above this standard there is an unlimited range of moral worth, up to the most exalted heroism, which should be fostered by every positive encouragement, though not converted into an obligation. It is as much a part of our scheme as of M. Comte's, that the direct cultivation of altruism, and the subordination of egoism to it, far beyond the point of absolute moral duty, should be one of the chief aims of education, both individual and collective. We even recognize the value, for this end, of ascetic discipline, in the original Greek sense of the word. We think with Dr Johnson, that he who has never denied himself anything which is not wrong, cannot be fully trusted for denying himself everything which is so. We do not doubt that children and young persons will one day be again systematically disciplined in self-mortification; that they will be taught, as in antiquity, to control their appetites, to brave dangers, and submit voluntarily to pain, as simple exercises in education. Something has been lost as well as gained by no longer giving to every citizen the training necessary for a soldier. Nor can any pains taken be too great, to form the habit, and develop the desire, of being useful to others and to the world, by the practice, independently of reward and of every personal consideration, of positive virtue beyond the bounds of prescribed duty. No efforts should be spared to associate the pupil's self-respect, and his desire of the respect of others, with service rendered to Humanity; when possible, collectively, but at all events, what is always possible, in the persons of its individual members. There are many remarks and precepts in M. Comte's volumes, which, as no less pertinent to our conception of morality than to his, we fully accept. For example; without admitting that to make "calculs personnels" is contrary to morality, we agree with him in the opinion, that the principal hygienic precepts should be inculcated, not solely or principally as maxims of prudence, but as a matter of duty to others, since by squandering our health we disable ourselves from rendering to our fellow-creatures the services to which they are entitled. As M. Comte truly says, the prudential motive is by no means fully sufficient for the purpose, even physicians often disregarding their own precepts. The personal penalties of neglect of health are commonly distant, as well as more or less uncertain, and require the additional and more immediate sanction of moral responsibility. M. Comte, therefore, in this instance, is, we conceive, right in principle; though we have not the smallest doubt that he would have gone into extreme exaggeration in practice, and would have wholly ignored the legitimate liberty of the individual to judge for himself respecting his own bodily conditions, with due relation to the sufficiency of his means of knowledge, and taking the responsibility of the result.

Connected with the same considerations is another idea of M. Comte, which has great beauty and grandeur in it, and the realization of which, within the bounds of possibility, would be a cultivation of the social feelings on a most essential point. It is, that every person who lives by any useful work, should be habituated to regard himself not as an individual working for his private benefit, but as a public functionary; and his wages, of whatever sort, as not the remuneration or purchase-money of his labour, which should be given freely, but as the provision made by society to enable him to carry it on, and to replace the materials and products which have been consumed in the process. M. Comte observes, that in modern industry every one in fact works much more for others than for himself, since his productions are to be consumed by others, and it is only necessary that his thoughts and imagination should adapt themselves to the real state of the fact. The practical problem, however, is not quite so simple, for a strong sense that he is working for others may lead to nothing better than feeling himself necessary to them, and instead of freely giving his commodity, may only encourage him to put a high price upon it. What M. Comte really means is that we should regard working for the benefit of others as a good in itself; that we should desire it for its own sake, and not for the sake of remuneration, which cannot justly be claimed for doing what we like: that the proper return for a service to society is the gratitude of society: and that the moral claim of any one in regard to the provision for his personal wants, is not a question of *quid pro quo* in respect to his co-operation, but of how much the circumstances of society permit to be assigned to him, consistently with the just claims of others. To this opinion we entirely subscribe. The rough method of settling the labourer's share of the produce, the competition of the market, may represent a practical necessity, but certainly not a moral ideal. Its defence is, that civilization has not hitherto been equal to organizing anything better than this first rude approach to an equitable distribution. Rude as it is, we for the present go less wrong by leaving the thing to settle itself, than by settling it artificially in any mode which has yet been tried. But in whatever manner that question may ultimately be decided, the true moral and social idea of Labour is in no way affected by it. Until labourers and employers perform the work of industry in the spirit in which soldiers perform that of an army, industry will never be moralized, and military life will remain, what, in spite of the anti-social character of its direct object, it has hitherto been—the chief school of moral co-operation.

Thus far of the general idea of M. Comte's ethics and religion. We must now say something of the details. Here we approach the ludicrous side of the subject: but we shall unfortunately have to relate other things far more really ridiculous.

There cannot be a religion without a *cultus*. We use this term for want of any other, for its nearest equivalent, worship, suggests a different order of ideas. We mean by it, a set of systematic observances, intended to cultivate and maintain the religious sentiment. Though M. Comte justly appreciates the superior efficacy of acts, in keeping up and strengthening the feeling which prompts them, over any mode whatever of mere expression, he takes pains to organize the latter also with great minuteness. He provides an equivalent both for the private devotions, and for the public ceremonies, of other faiths. The reader will be surprised to learn, that the former consists of prayer. But prayer, as understood by M. Comte, does not mean asking; it is a mere outpouring of feeling; and for this view of it he claims the authority of the Christian mystics. It is not to be addressed to the Grand Etre, to collective Humanity; though he occasionally carries metaphor so far as to style this a goddess. The honours to collective Humanity are reserved for the public celebrations. Private adoration is to be addressed to it in the persons of worthy individual representatives, who may be either living or dead, but must in all cases be women; for women, being the *sexe aimant*, represent the best attribute of humanity, that which ought to regulate all human life, nor can Humanity possibly be symbolized in any form but that of a woman. The objects of private adoration are the mother, the wife, and the daughter, representing severally the past, the present, and the future, and calling into active exercise the three social sentiments, veneration, attachment, and kindness. We are to regard them, whether dead or alive, as our guardian angels, "les vrais anges gardiens." If the last two have never existed, or if, in the particular case, any of the three types is too faulty for the office assigned to it, their place may be supplied by some other type of womanly excellence, even by one merely historical. Be the object living or dead, the adoration (as we understand it) is to be addressed only to the idea. The prayer consists of two parts; a commemoration, followed by an effusion. By a commemoration M. Comte means an effort of memory and imagination, summoning up with the utmost possible vividness the image of the object: and every artifice is exhausted to render the image as life-like, as close to the reality, as near an approach to actual hallucination, as is consistent with sanity. This degree of intensity having been, as far as practicable, attained, the effusion follows. Every person should compose his own form of prayer, which should be repeated not mentally only, but orally, and may be added to or varied for sufficient cause, but never arbitrarily. It may be interspersed with passages from the best poets, when they present themselves spontaneously, as giving a felicitous expression to the adorer's own feeling. These observances M. Comte practised to the memory of his Clotilde, and he enjoins them on all true believers. They are to occupy two hours of every day, divided into three parts; at rising, in the middle of the working hours, and in bed at night. The first, which should be in a kneeling attitude, will commonly be the longest, and the second the shortest. The third is to be extended as nearly as possible to the moment of falling asleep, that its effect may be felt in disciplining even the dreams.

 The public *cultus* consists of a series of celebrations or festivals, eighty-four in the year, so arranged that at least one occurs in every week. They are devoted to the successive glorification of Humanity itself; of the various ties, political and domestic, among mankind; of the successive stages in the past evolution of our species; and of the several classes into which M. Comte's polity divides mankind. M. Comte's religion has, moreover, nine Sacraments; consisting in the solemn consecration, by the priests of Humanity, with appropriate exhortations, of all the great transitions in life; the entry into life itself, and into each of its successive stages: education, marriage, the choice of a profession, and so forth. Among these is death, which receives the name of transformation, and is considered as a passage from objective existence to subjective—to living in the memory of our fellow-creatures. Having no eternity of objective existence to offer, M. Comte's religion gives it all he can, by holding out the hope of subjective immortality—of existing in the remembrance and in the posthumous adoration of mankind at large, if we have done anything to deserve remembrance from them; at all events, of those whom we loved during life; and when they too are gone, of being included in the collective adoration paid to the Grand Etre. People are to be taught to look forward to this as a sufficient recompense for the devotion of a whole life to the service of Humanity. Seven years after death, comes the last Sacrament: a public judgment, by the priesthood, on the memory of the defunct. This is not designed for purposes of reprobation, but of honour, and any one may, by declaration during life, exempt himself from it. If judged, and found worthy, he is solemnly incorporated with the Grand Etre, and his remains are transferred from the civil to the religious place of sepulture: "le bois sacré" qui doit entourer chaque temple de l'Humanité."

This brief abstract gives no idea of the minuteness of M. Comte's prescriptions, and the extraordinary height to which he carries the mania for regulation by which Frenchmen are distinguished among Europeans, and M. Comte among Frenchmen. It is this which throws an irresistible air of ridicule over the whole subject. There is nothing really ridiculous in the devotional practices which M. Comte recommends towards a cherished memory or an ennobling ideal, when they come unprompted from the depths of the individual feeling; but there is something ineffably ludicrous in enjoining that everybody shall practise them three times daily for a period of two hours, not because his feelings require them, but for the premeditated, purpose of getting his feelings up. The ludicrous, however, in any of its shapes, is a phaenomenon with which M. Comte seems to have been totally unacquainted. There is nothing in his writings from which it could be inferred that he knew of the existence of such things as wit and humour. The only writer distinguished for either, of whom he shows any admiration, is Molière, and him he admires not for his wit but for his wisdom. We notice this without intending any reflection on M. Comte; for a profound conviction raises a person above the feeling of ridicule. But there are passages in his writings which, it really seems to us, could have been written by no man who had ever laughed. We will give one of these instances. Besides the regular prayers, M. Comte's religion, like the Catholic, has need of forms which can be applied to casual and unforeseen occasions. These, he says, must in general be left to the believer's own choice; but he suggests as a very suitable one the repetition of "the fundamental formula of Positivism," viz., "l'amour pour principe, l'ordre pour base, et le progrès pour but." Not content, however, with an equivalent for the Paters and Aves of Catholicism, he must have one for the sign of the cross also; and he thus delivers himself:[23] "Cette expansion peut être perfectionnée par des signes universels.... Afin de mieux développer l'aptitude nécessaire de la formule positiviste à représenter toujours la condition humaine, il convient ordinairement de l'énoncer en touchant successivement les principaux organes que la théorie cérébrale assigne à ses trois éléments." This *may* be a very appropriate mode of expressing one's devotion to the Grand Etre: but any one who had appreciated its effect on the profane reader, would have thought it judicious to keep it back till a considerably more advanced stage in the propagation of the Positive Religion.

As M. Comte's religion has a *cultus*, so also it has a clergy, who are the pivot of his entire social and political system. Their nature and office will be best shown by describing his ideal of political society in its normal state, with the various classes of which it is composed.

The necessity of a Spiritual Power, distinct and separate from the temporal government, is the essential principle of M. Comte's political scheme; as it may well be, since the Spiritual Power is the only counterpoise he provides or tolerates, to the absolute dominion of the civil rulers. Nothing can exceed his combined detestation and contempt for government by assemblies, and for parliamentary or representative institutions in any form. They are an expedient, in his opinion, only suited to a state of transition, and even that nowhere but in England. The attempt to naturalize them in France, or any Continental nation, he regards as mischievous quackery. Louis Napoleon's usurpation is absolved, is made laudable to him, because it overthrew a representative government. Election of superiors by inferiors, except as a revolutionary expedient, is an abomination in his sight. Public functionaries of all kinds should name their successors, subject to the approbation of their own superiors, and giving public notice of the nomination so long beforehand as to admit of discussion, and the timely revocation of a wrong choice. But, by the side of the temporal rulers, he places another authority, with no power to command, but only to advise and remonstrate. The family being, in his mind as in that of Frenchmen generally, the foundation and essential type of all society, the separation of the two powers commences there. The spiritual, or moral and religious power, in a family, is the women of it. The positivist family is composed of the "fundamental couple," their children, and the parents of the man, if alive. The whole government of the household, except as regards the education of the children, resides in the man; and even over that he has complete power, but should forbear to exert it. The part assigned to the women is to improve the man through his affections, and to bring up the children, who, until the age of fourteen, at which scientific instruction begins, are to be educated wholly by their mother. That women may be better fitted for these functions, they are peremptorily excluded from all others. No woman is to work for her living. Every woman is to be supported by her husband or her male relations, and if she has none of these, by the State. She is to have no powers of government, even domestic, and no property. Her legal rights of inheritance are preserved to her, that her feelings of duty may make her voluntarily forego them. There are to be no marriage portions, that women may no longer be sought in marriage from interested motives. Marriages are to be rigidly indissoluble, except for a single cause. It is remarkable that the bitterest enemy of divorce among all philosophers, nevertheless allows it, in a case which the laws of England, and of other countries reproached by him with tolerating divorce, do not admit: namely, when one of the parties has been sentenced to an infamizing punishment, involving loss of civil rights. It is monstrous that condemnation, even for life, to a felon's punishment, should leave an unhappy victim bound to, and in the wife's case under the legal authority of, the culprit. M. Comte could feel for the injustice in this special case, because it chanced to be the unfortunate situation of his Clotilde. Minor degrees of unworthiness may entitle the innocent party to a legal separation, but without the power of re-marriage. Second marriages, indeed, are not permitted by the Positive Religion. There is to be no impediment to them by law, but morality is to condemn them, and every couple who are married religiously as well as civilly are to make a vow of eternal widowhood, "le veuvage éternel." This absolute monogamy is, in M. Comte's opinion, essential to the complete fusion between two beings, which is the essence of marriage; and moreover, eternal constancy is required by the posthumous adoration, which is to be continuously paid by the survivor to one who, though objectively dead, still lives "subjectively." The domestic spiritual power, which resides in the women of the family, is chiefly concentrated in the most venerable of them, the husband's mother, while alive. It has an auxiliary in the influence of age, represented by the husband's father, who is supposed to have passed the period of retirement from active life, fixed by M. Comte (for he fixes everything) at sixty-three; at which age the head of the family gives up the reins of authority to his son, retaining only a consultative voice.

This domestic Spiritual Power, being principally moral, and confined to a private life, requires the support and guidance of an intellectual power exterior to it, the sphere of which will naturally be wider, extending also to public life. This consists of the clergy, or priesthood, for M. Comte is fond of borrowing the consecrated expressions of Catholicism to denote the nearest equivalents which his own system affords. The clergy are the theoretic or philosophical class, and are supported by an endowment from the State, voted periodically, but administered by themselves. Like women, they are to be excluded from all riches, and from all participation in power (except the absolute power of each over his own household). They are neither to inherit, nor to receive emolument from any of their functions, or from their writings or teachings of any description, but are to live solely on their small salaries. This M. Comte deems necessary to the complete disinterestedness of their counsel. To have the confidence of the masses, they must, like the masses, be poor. Their exclusion from political and from all other practical occupations is indispensable for the same reason, and for others equally peremptory. Those occupations are, he contends, incompatible with the habits of mind necessary to philosophers. A practical position, either private or public, chains the mind to specialities and details, while a philosopher's business is with general truths and connected views (vues d'ensemble). These, again, require an habitual abstraction from details, which unfits the mind for judging well and rapidly of individual cases. The same person cannot be both a good theorist and a good practitioner or ruler, though practitioners and rulers ought to have a solid theoretic education. The two kinds of function must be absolutely exclusive of one another: to attempt them both, is inconsistent with fitness for either. But as men may mistake their vocation, up to the age of thirty-five they are allowed to change their career.

To the clergy is entrusted the theoretic or scientific instruction of youth. The medical art also is to be in their hands, since no one is fit to be a physician who does not study and understand the whole man, moral as well as physical. M. Comte has a contemptuous opinion of the existing race of physicians, who, he says, deserve no higher name than that of veterinaires, since they concern themselves with man only in his animal, and not in his human character. In his last years, M. Comte (as we learn from Dr Robinet's volume) indulged in the wildest speculations on medical science, declaring all maladies to be one and the same disease, the disturbance or destruction of "l'unité cérébrale." The other functions of the clergy are moral, much more than intellectual. They are the spiritual directors, and venerated advisers, of the active or practical classes, including the political. They are the mediators in all social differences; between the labourers, for instance, and their employers. They are to advise and admonish on all important violations of the moral law. Especially, it devolves on them to keep the rich and powerful to the performance of their moral duties towards their inferiors. If private remonstrance fails, public denunciation is to follow: in extreme cases they may proceed to the length of excommunication, which, though it only operates through opinion, yet if it carries opinion with it, may, as M. Comte complacently observes, be of such powerful efficacy, that the richest man may be driven to produce his subsistence by his own manual labour, through the impossibility of inducing any other person to work for him. In this as in all other cases, the priesthood depends for its authority on carrying with it the mass of the people—those who, possessing no accumulations, live on the wages of daily labour; popularly but incorrectly termed the working classes, and by French writers, in their Roman law phraseology, proletaires. These, therefore, who are not allowed the smallest political rights, are incorporated into the Spiritual Power, of which they form, after women and the clergy, the third element.

It remains to give an account of the Temporal Power, composed of the rich and the employers of labour, two classes who in M. Comte's system are reduced to one, for he allows of no idle rich. A life made up of mere amusement and self-indulgence, though not interdicted by law, is to be deemed so disgraceful, that nobody with the smallest sense of shame would choose to be guilty of it. Here, we think, M. Comte has lighted on a true principle, towards which the tone of opinion in modern Europe is more and more tending, and which is destined to be one of the constitutive principles of regenerated society. We believe, for example, with him, that in the future there will be no class of landlords living at ease on their rents, but every landlord will be a capitalist trained to agriculture, himself superintending and directing the cultivation of his estate. No one but he who guides the work, should have the control of the tools. In M. Comte's system, the rich, as a rule, consist of the "captains of industry:" but the rule is not entirely without exception, for M. Comte recognizes other useful modes of employing riches. In particular, one of his favourite ideas is that of an order of Chivalry, composed of the most generous and self-devoted of the rich, voluntarily dedicating themselves, like knights-errant of old, to the redressing of wrongs, and the protection of the weak and oppressed. He remarks, that oppression, in modern life, can seldom reach, or even venture to attack, the life or liberty of its victims (he forgets the case of domestic tyranny), but only their pecuniary means, and it is therefore by the purse chiefly that individuals can usefully interpose, as they formerly did by the sword. The occupation, however, of nearly all the rich, will be the direction of labour, and for this work they will be educated. Reciprocally, it is in M. Comte's opinion essential, that all directors of labour should be rich. Capital (in which he includes land) should be concentrated in a few holders, so that every capitalist may conduct the most extensive operations which one mind is capable of superintending. This is not only demanded by good economy, in order to take the utmost advantage of a rare kind of practical ability, but it necessarily follows from the principle of M. Comte's scheme, which regards a capitalist as a public functionary. M. Comte's conception of the relation of capital to society is essentially that of Socialists, but he would bring about by education and opinion, what they aim at effecting by positive institution. The owner of capital is by no means to consider himself its absolute proprietor. Legally he is not to be controlled in his dealings with it, for power should be in proportion to responsibility: but it does not belong to him for his own use; he is merely entrusted by society with a portion of the accumulations made by the past providence of mankind, to be administered for the benefit of the present generation and of posterity, under the obligation of preserving them unimpaired, and handing them down, more or less augmented, to our successors. He is not entitled to dissipate them, or divert them from the service of Humanity to his own pleasures. Nor has he a moral right to consume on himself the whole even of his profits. He is bound in conscience, if they exceed his reasonable wants, to employ the surplus in improving either the efficiency of his operations, or the physical and mental condition of his labourers. The portion of his gains which he may appropriate to his own use, must be decided by himself, under accountability to opinion; and opinion ought not to look very narrowly into the matter, nor hold him to a rigid reckoning for any moderate indulgence of luxury or ostentation; since under the great responsibilities that will be imposed on him, the position of an employer of labour will be so much less desirable, to any one in whom the instincts of pride and vanity are not strong, than the "heureuse insouciance" of a labourer, that those instincts must be to a certain degree indulged, or no one would undertake the office. With this limitation, every employer is a mere administrator of his possessions, for his work-people and for society at large. If he indulges himself lavishly, without reserving an ample remuneration for all who are employed under him, he is morally culpable, and will incur sacerdotal admonition. This state of things necessarily implies that capital should be in few hands, because, as M. Comte observes, without great riches, the obligations which society ought to impose, could not be fulfilled without an amount of personal abnegation that it would be hopeless to expect. If a person is conspicuously qualified for the conduct of an industrial enterprise, but destitute of the fortune necessary for undertaking it, M. Comte recommends that he should be enriched by subscription, or, in cases of sufficient importance, by the State. Small landed proprietors and capitalists, and the middle classes altogether, he regards as a parasitic growth, destined to disappear, the best of the body becoming large capitalists, and the remainder proletaires. Society will consist only of rich and poor, and it will be the business of the rich to make the best possible lot for the poor. The remuneration of the labourers will continue, as at present, to be a matter of voluntary arrangement between them and their employers, the last resort on either side being refusal of co-operation, "refus de concours," in other words, a strike or a lock-out; with the sacerdotal order for mediators in case of need. But though wages are to be an affair of free contract, their standard is not to be the competition of the market, but the application of the products in equitable proportion between the wants of the labourers and the wants and dignity of the employer. As it is one of M. Comte's principles that a question cannot be usefully proposed without an attempt at a solution, he gives his ideas from the beginning as to what the normal income of a labouring family should be. They are on such a scale, that until some great extension shall have taken place in the scientific resources of mankind, it is no wonder he thinks it necessary to limit as much as possible the number of those who are to be supported by what is left of the produce. In the first place the labourer's dwelling, which is to consist of seven rooms, is, with all that it contains, to be his own property: it is the only landed property he is allowed to possess, but every family should be the absolute owner of all things which are destined for its exclusive use. Lodging being thus independently provided for, and education and medical attendance being secured gratuitously by the general arrangements of society, the pay of the labourer is to consist of two portions, the one monthly, and of fixed amount, the other weekly, and proportioned to the produce of his labour. The former M. Comte fixes at 100 francs (£4) for a month of 28 days; being £52 a year: and the rate of piece-work should be such as to make the other part amount to an average of seven francs (5 *s.* 6*d.*) per working day.

Agreeably to M. Comte's rule, that every public functionary should appoint his successor, the capitalist has unlimited power of transmitting his capital by gift or bequest, after his own death or retirement. In general it will be best bestowed entire upon one person, unless the business will advantageously admit of subdivision. He will naturally leave it to one or more of his sons, if sufficiently qualified; and rightly so, hereditary being, in M. Comte's opinion, preferable to acquired wealth, as being usually more generously administered. But, merely as his sons, they have no moral right to it. M. Comte here recognizes another of the principles, on which we believe that the constitution of regenerated society will rest. He maintains (as others in the present generation have done) that the father owes nothing to his son, except a good education, and pecuniary aid sufficient for an advantageous start in life: that he is entitled, and may be morally bound, to leave the bulk of his fortune to some other properly selected person or persons, whom he judges likely to make a more beneficial use of it. This is the first of three important points, in which M. Comte's theory of the family, wrong as we deem it in its foundations, is in advance of prevailing theories and existing institutions. The second is the re-introduction of adoption, not only in default of children, but to fulfil the purposes, and satisfy the sympathetic wants, to which such children as there are may happen to be inadequate. The third is a most important point—the incorporation of domestics as substantive members of the family. There is hardly any part of the present constitution of society more essentially vicious, and morally injurious to both parties, than the relation between masters and servants. To make this a really human and a moral relation, is one of the principal desiderata in social improvement. The feeling of the vulgar of all classes, that domestic service has anything in it peculiarly mean, is a feeling than which there is none meaner. In the feudal ages, youthful nobles of the highest rank thought themselves honoured by officiating in what is now called a menial capacity, about the persons of superiors of both sexes, for whom they felt respect: and, as M. Comte observes, there are many families who can in no other way so usefully serve Humanity, as by ministering to the bodily wants of other families, called to functions which require the devotion of all their thoughts. "We will add, by way of supplement to M. Comte's doctrine, that much of the daily physical work of a household, even in opulent families, if silly notions of degradation, common to all ranks, did not interfere, might very advantageously be performed by the family itself, at least by its younger members; to whom it would give healthful exercise of the bodily powers, which has now to be sought in modes far less useful, and also a familiar acquaintance with the real work of the world, and a moral willingness to take their share of its burthens, which, in the great majority of the better-off classes, do not now get cultivated at all.

We have still to speak of the directly political functions of the rich, or, as M. Comte terms them, the patriciate. The entire political government is to be in their hands. First, however, the existing nations are to be broken up into small republics, the largest not exceeding the size of Belgium, Portugal, or Tuscany; any larger nationalities being incompatible with the unity of wants and feelings, which is required, not only to give due strength to the sentiment of patriotism (always strongest in small states), but to prevent undue compression; for no territory, M. Comte thinks, can without oppression be governed from a distant centre. Algeria, therefore, is to be given up to the Arabs, Corsica to its inhabitants, and France proper is to be, before the end of the century, divided into seventeen republics, corresponding to the number of considerable towns: Paris, however, (need it be said?) succeeding to Rome as the religious metropolis of the world. Ireland, Scotland, and Wales, are to be separated from England, which is of course to detach itself from all its transmarine dependencies. In each state thus constituted, the powers of government are to be vested in a triumvirate of the three principal bankers, who are to take the foreign, home, and financial departments respectively. How they are to conduct the government and remain bankers, does not clearly appear; but it must be intended that they should combine both offices, for they are to receive no pecuniary remuneration for the political one. Their power is to amount to a dictatorship (M. Comte's own word): and he is hardly justified in saying that he gives political power to the rich, since he gives it over the rich and every one else, to three individuals of the number, not even chosen by the rest, but named by their predecessors. As a check on the dictators, there is to be complete freedom of speech, writing, printing, and voluntary association; and all important acts of the government, except in cases of emergency, are to be announced sufficiently long beforehand to ensure ample discussion. This, and the influences of the Spiritual Power, are the only guarantees provided against misgovernment. When we consider that the complete dominion of every nation of mankind is thus handed over to only four men—for the Spiritual Power is to be under the absolute and undivided control of a single Pontiff for the whole human race—one is appalled at the picture of entire subjugation and slavery, which is recommended to us as the last and highest result of the evolution of Humanity. But the conception rises to the terrific, when we are told the mode in which the single High Priest of Humanity is intended to use his authority. It is the most warning example we know, into what frightful aberrations a powerful and comprehensive mind may be led by the exclusive following out of a single idea.

The single idea of M. Comte, on this subject, is that the intellect should be wholly subordinated to the feelings; or, to translate the meaning out of sentimental into logical language, that the exercise of the intellect, as of all our other faculties, should have for its sole object the general good. Every other employment of it should be accounted not only idle and frivolous, but morally culpable. Being indebted wholly to Humanity for the cultivation to which we owe our mental powers, we are bound in return to consecrate them wholly to her service. Having made up his mind that this ought to be, there is with M. Comte but one step to concluding that the Grand Pontiff of Humanity must take care that it shall be; and on this foundation he organizes an elaborate system for the total suppression of all independent thought. He does not, indeed, invoke the arm of the law, or call for any prohibitions. The clergy are to have no monopoly. Any one else may cultivate science if he can, may write and publish if he can find readers, may give private instruction if anybody consents to receive it. But since the sacerdotal body will absorb into itself all but those whom it deems either intellectually or morally unequal to the vocation, all rival teachers will, as he calculates, be so discredited beforehand, that their competition will not be formidable. Within the body itself, the High Priest has it in his power to make sure that there shall be no opinions, and no exercise of mind, but such as he approves; for he alone decides the duties and local residence of all its members, and can even eject them from the body. Before electing to be under this rule, we feel a natural curiosity to know in what manner it is to be exercised. Humanity has only yet had one Pontiff, whose mental qualifications for the post are not likely to be often surpassed, M. Comte himself. It is of some importance to know what are the ideas of this High Priest, concerning the moral and religious government of the human intellect.

One of the doctrines which M. Comte most strenuously enforces in his later writings is, that during the preliminary evolution of humanity, terminated by the foundation of Positivism, the free development of our forces of all kinds was the important matter, but that from this time forward the principal need is to regulate them. Formerly the danger was of their being insufficient, but henceforth, of their being abused. Let us express, in passing, our entire dissent from this doctrine. Whoever thinks that the wretched education which mankind as yet receive, calls forth their mental powers (except those of a select few) in a sufficient or even tolerable degree, must be very easily satisfied: and the abuse of them, far from becoming proportionally greater as knowledge and mental capacity increase, becomes rapidly less, provided always that the diffusion of those qualities keeps pace with their growth. The abuse of intellectual power is only to be dreaded, when society is divided between a few highly cultivated intellects and an ignorant and stupid multitude. But mental power is a thing which M. Comte does not want—or wants infinitely less than he wants submission and obedience. Of all the ingredients of human nature, he continually says, the intellect most needs to be disciplined and reined-in. It is the most turbulent "le plus perturbateur," of all the mental elements; more so than even the selfish instincts. Throughout the whole modern transition, beginning with ancient Greece (for M. Comte tells us that we have always been in a state of revolutionary transition since then), the intellect has been in a state of systematic insurrection against "le coeur." The metaphysicians and literati (lettrés), after helping to pull down the old religion and social order, are rootedly hostile to the construction of the new, and desiring only to prolong the existing scepticism and intellectual anarchy, which secure to them a cheap social ascendancy, without the labour of earning it by solid scientific preparation. The scientific class, from whom better might have been expected, are, if possible, worse. Void of enlarged views, despising all that is too large for their comprehension, devoted exclusively each to his special science, contemptuously indifferent to moral and political interests, their sole aim is to acquire an easy reputation, and in France (through paid Academies and professorships) personal lucre, by pushing their sciences into idle and useless inquiries (speculations oiseuses), of no value to the real interests of mankind, and tending to divert the thoughts from them. One of the duties most incumbent on opinion and on the Spiritual Power, is to stigmatize as immoral, and effectually suppress, these useless employments of the speculative faculties. All exercise of thought should be abstained from, which has not some beneficial tendency, some actual utility to mankind. M. Comte, of course, is not the man to say that it must be a merely material utility. If a speculation, though it has no doctrinal, has a logical value—if it throws any light on universal Method—it is still more deserving of cultivation than if its usefulness was merely practical: but, either as method or as doctrine, it must bring forth fruits to Humanity, otherwise it is not only contemptible, but criminal.

That there is a portion of truth at the bottom of all this, we should be the last to deny. No respect is due to any employment of the intellect which does not tend to the good of mankind. It is precisely on a level with any idle amusement, and should be condemned as waste of time, if carried beyond the limit within which amusement is permissible. And whoever devotes powers of thought which could render to Humanity services it urgently needs, to speculations and studies which it could dispense with, is liable to the discredit attaching to a well-grounded suspicion of caring little for Humanity. But who can affirm positively of any speculations, guided by right scientific methods, on subjects really accessible to the human faculties, that they are incapable of being of any use? Nobody knows what knowledge will prove to be of use, and what is destined to be useless. The most that can be said is that some kinds are of more certain, and above all, of more present utility than others. How often the most important practical results have been the remote consequence of studies which no one would have expected to lead to them! Could the mathematicians, who, in the schools of Alexandria, investigated the properties of the ellipse, have foreseen that nearly two thousand years afterwards their speculations would explain the solar system, and a little later would enable ships safely to circumnavigate the earth? Even in M. Comte's opinion, it is well for mankind that, in those early days, knowledge was thought worth pursuing for its own sake. Nor has the "foundation of Positivism," we imagine, so far changed the conditions of human existence, that it should now be criminal to acquire, by observation and reasoning, a knowledge of the facts of the universe, leaving to posterity to find a use for it. Even in the last two or three years, has not the discovery of new metals, which may prove important even in the practical arts, arisen from one of the investigations which M. Comte most unequivocally condemns as idle, the research into the internal constitution of the sun? How few, moreover, of the discoveries which have changed the face of the world, either were or could have been arrived at by investigations aiming directly at the object! Would the mariner's compass ever have been found by direct efforts for the improvement of navigation? Should we have reached the electric telegraph by any amount of striving for a means of instantaneous communication, if Franklin had not identified electricity with lightning, and Ampère with magnetism? The most apparently insignificant archaeological or geological fact, is often found to throw a light on human history, which M. Comte, the basis of whose social philosophy is history, should be the last person to disparage. The direction of the entrance to the three great Pyramids of Ghizeh, by showing the position of the circumpolar stars at the time when they were built, is the best evidence we even now have of the immense antiquity of Egyptian civilization.[24] The one point on which M. Comte's doctrine has some colour of reason, is the case of sidereal astronomy: so little knowledge of it being really accessible to us, and the connexion of that little with any terrestrial interests being, according to all our means of judgment, infinitesimal. It is certainly difficult to imagine how any considerable benefit to humanity can be derived from a knowledge of the motions of the double stars: should these ever become important to us it will be in so prodigiously remote an age, that we can afford to remain ignorant of them until, at least, all our moral, political, and social difficulties have been settled. Yet the discovery that gravitation extends even to those remote regions, gives some additional strength to the conviction of the universality of natural laws; and the habitual meditation on such vast objects and distances is not without an aesthetic usefulness, by kindling and exalting the imagination, the worth of which in itself, and even its re-action on the intellect, M. Comte is quite capable of appreciating. He would reply, however, that there are better means of accomplishing these purposes. In the same spirit he condemns the study even of the solar system, when extended to any planets but those which are visible to the naked eye, and which alone exert an appreciable gravitative influence on the earth. Even the perturbations he thinks it idle to study, beyond a mere general conception of them, and thinks that astronomy may well limit its domain to the motions and mutual action of the earth, sun, and moon. He looks for a similar expurgation of all the other sciences. In one passage he expressly says that the greater part of the researches which are really accessible to us are idle and useless. He would pare down the dimensions of all the sciences as narrowly as possible. He is continually repeating that no science, as an abstract study, should be carried further than is necessary to lay the foundation for the science next above it, and so ultimately for moral science, the principal purpose of them all. Any further extension of the mathematical and physical sciences should be merely "episodic;" limited to what may from time to time be demanded by the requirements of industry and the arts; and should be left to the industrial classes, except when they find it necessary to apply to the sacerdotal order for some additional development of scientific theory. This, he evidently thinks, would be a rare contingency, most physical truths sufficiently concrete and real for practice being empirical. Accordingly in estimating the number of clergy necessary for France, Europe, and our entire planet (for his forethought extends thus far), he proportions it solely to their moral and religious attributions (overlooking, by the way, even their medical); and leaves nobody with any time to cultivate the sciences, except abortive candidates for the priestly office, who having been refused admittance into it for insufficiency in moral excellence or in strength of character, may be thought worth retaining as "pensioners" of the sacerdotal order, on account of their theoretic abilities.

It is no exaggeration to say, that M. Comte gradually acquired a real hatred for scientific and all purely intellectual pursuits, and was bent on retaining no more of them than was strictly indispensable. The greatest of his anxieties is lest people should reason, and seek to know, more than enough. He regards all abstraction and all reasoning as morally dangerous, by developing an inordinate pride (orgueil), and still more, by producing dryness (scheresse). Abstract thought, he says, is not a wholesome occupation for more than a small number of human beings, nor of them for more than a small part of their time. Art, which calls the emotions into play along with and more than the reason, is the only intellectual exercise really adapted to human nature. It is nevertheless indispensable that the chief theories of the various abstract sciences, together with the modes in which those theories were historically and logically arrived at, should form a part of universal education: for, first, it is only thus that the methods can be learnt, by which to attain the results sought by the moral and social sciences: though we cannot perceive that M. Comte got at his own moral and social results by those processes. Secondly, the principal truths of the subordinate sciences are necessary to the systematization (still systematization!) of our conceptions, by binding together our notions of the world in a set of propositions, which are coherent, and are a sufficiently correct representation of fact for our practical wants. Thirdly, a familiar knowledge of the invariable laws of natural phaenomena is a great elementary lesson of submission, which, he is never weary of saying, is the first condition both of morality and of happiness. For these reasons, he would cause to be taught, from the age of fourteen to that of twenty-one, to all persons, rich and poor, girls or youths, a knowledge of the whole series of abstract sciences, such as none but the most highly instructed persons now possess, and of a far more systematic and philosophical character than is usually possessed even by them. (N.B.—They are to learn, during the same years, Greek and Latin, having previously, between the ages of seven and fourteen, learnt the five principal modern languages, to the degree necessary for reading, with due appreciation, the chief poetical compositions in each.) But they are to be taught all this, not only without encouraging, but stifling as much as possible, the examining and questioning spirit. The disposition which should be encouraged is that of receiving all on the authority of the teacher. The Positivist faith, even in its scientific part, is *la foi démontrable*, but ought by no means to be *la foi toujours démontrée*. The pupils have no business to be over-solicitous about proof. The teacher should not even present the proofs to them in a complete form, or as proofs. The object of instruction is to make them understand the doctrines themselves, perceive their mutual connexion, and form by means of them a consistent and *systematized* conception of nature. As for the demonstrations, it is rather desirable than otherwise that even theorists should forget them, retaining only the results. Among all the aberrations of scientific men, M. Comte thinks none greater than the pedantic anxiety they show for complete proof, and perfect rationalization of scientific processes. It ought to be enough that the doctrines afford an explanation of phaenomena, consistent with itself and with known facts, and that the processes are justified by their fruits. This over-anxiety for proof, he complains, is breaking down, by vain scruples, the knowledge which seemed to have been attained; witness the present state of chemistry. The demand of proof for what has been accepted by Humanity, is itself a mark of "distrust, if not hostility, to the sacerdotal order" (the naïveté of this would be charming, if it were not deplorable), and is a revolt against the traditions of the human race. So early had the new High Priest adopted the feelings and taken up the inheritance of the old. One of his favourite aphorisms is the strange one, that the living are more and more governed by the dead. As is not uncommon with him, he introduces the dictum in one sense, and uses it in another. What he at first means by it, is that as civilization advances, the sum of our possessions, physical and intellectual, is due in a decreasing proportion to ourselves, and in an increasing one to our progenitors. The use he makes of it is, that we should submit ourselves more and more implicitly to the authority of previous generations, and suffer ourselves less and less to doubt their judgment, or test by our own reason the grounds of their opinions. The unwillingness of the human intellect and conscience, in their present state of "anarchy," to sign their own abdication, lie calls "the insurrection of the living against the dead." To this complexion has Positive Philosophy come at last!

Worse, however, remains to be told. M. Comte selects a hundred volumes of science, philosophy, poetry, history, and general knowledge, which he deems a sufficient library for every positivist, even of the theoretic order, and actually proposes a systematic holocaust of books in general—it would almost seem of all books except these. Even that to which he shows most indulgence, poetry, except the very best, is to undergo a similar fate, with the reservation of select passages, on the ground that, poetry being intended to cultivate our instinct of ideal perfection, any kind of it that is less than the best is worse than none. This imitation of the error, we will call it the crime, of the early Christians—and in an exaggerated form, for even they destroyed only those writings of pagans or heretics which were directed against themselves—is the one thing in M. Comte's projects which merits real indignation. When once M. Comte has decided, all evidence on the other side, nay, the very historical evidence on which he grounded his decision, had better perish. When mankind have enlisted under his banner, they must burn their ships. There is, though in a less offensive form, the same overweening presumption in a suggestion he makes, that all species of animals and plants which are useless to man should be systematically rooted out. As if any one could presume to assert that the smallest weed may not, as knowledge advances, be found to have some property serviceable to man. When we consider that the united power of the whole human race cannot reproduce a species once eradicated —that what is once done, in the extirpation of races, can never be repaired; one can only be thankful that amidst all which the past rulers of mankind have to answer for, they have never come up to the measure of the great regenerator of Humanity; mankind have not yet been under the rule of one who assumes that he knows all there is to be known, and that when he has put himself at the head of humanity, the book of human knowledge may be closed.

Of course M. Comte does not make this assumption consistently. He does not imagine that he actually possesses all knowledge, but only that he is an infallible judge what knowledge is worth possessing. He does not believe that mankind have reached in all directions the extreme limits of useful and laudable scientific inquiry. He thinks there is a large scope for it still, in adding to our power over the external world, but chiefly in perfecting our own physical, intellectual, and moral nature. He holds that all our mental strength should be economized, for the pursuit of this object in the mode leading most directly to the end. With this view, some one problem should always be selected, the solution of which would be more important than any other to the interests of humanity, and upon this the entire intellectual resources of the theoretic mind should be concentrated, until it is either resolved, or has to be given up as insoluble: after which mankind should go on to another, to be pursued with similar exclusiveness. The selection of this problem of course rests with the sacerdotal order, or in other words, with the High Priest. We should then see the whole speculative intellect of the human race simultaneously at work on one question, by orders from above, as a French minister of public instruction once boasted that a million of boys were saying the same lesson during the same half-hour in every town and village of France. The reader will be anxious to know, how much better and more wisely the human intellect will be applied under this absolute monarchy, and to what degree this system of government will be preferable to the present anarchy, in which every theorist does what is intellectually right in his own eyes. M. Comte has not left us in ignorance on this point. He gives us ample means of judging. The Pontiff of Positivism informs us what problem, in his opinion, should be selected before all others for this united pursuit.

What this problem is, we must leave those who are curious on the subject to learn from the treatise itself. When they have done so, they will be qualified to form their own opinion of the amount of advantage which the general good of mankind would be likely to derive, from exchanging the present "dispersive speciality" and "intellectual anarchy" for the subordination of the intellect to the *coeur*, personified in a High Priest, prescribing a single problem for the undivided study of the theoretic mind.

We have given a sufficient general idea of M. Comte's plan for the regeneration of human society, by putting an end to anarchy, and "systematizing" human thought and conduct under the direction of feeling. But an adequate conception will not have been formed of the height of his self-confidence, until something more has been told. Be it known, then, that M. Comte by no means proposes this new constitution of society for realization in the remote future. A complete plan of measures of transition is ready prepared, and he determines the year, before the end of the present century, in which the new spiritual and temporal powers will be installed, and the regime of our maturity will begin. He did not indeed calculate on converting to Positivism, within that time, more than a thousandth part of all the heads of families in Western Europe and its offshoots beyond the

Atlantic. But he fixes the time necessary for the complete political establishment of Positivism at thirty-three years, divided into three periods, of seven, five, and twenty-one years respectively. At the expiration of seven, the direction of public education in France would be placed in M. Comte's hands. In five years more, the Emperor Napoleon, or his successor, will resign his power to a provisional triumvirate, composed of three eminent proletaires of the positivist faith; for proletaires, though not fit for permanent rule, are the best agents of the transition, being the most free from the prejudices which are the chief obstacle to it. These rulers will employ the remaining twenty-one years in preparing society for its final constitution; and after duly installing the Spiritual Power, and effecting the decomposition of France into the seventeen republics before mentioned, will give over the temporal government of each to the normal dictatorship of the three bankers. A man may be deemed happy, but scarcely modest, who had such boundless confidence in his own powers of foresight, and expected so complete a triumph of his own ideas on the reconstitution of society within the possible limits of his lifetime. If he could live (he said) to the age of Pontenelle, or of Hobbes, or even of Voltaire, he should see all this realized, or as good as realized. He died, however, at sixty, without leaving any disciple sufficiently advanced to be appointed his successor. There is now a College, and a Director, of Positivism; but Humanity no longer possesses a High Priest.

What more remains to be said may be despatched more summarily. Its interest is philosophic rather than practical. In his four volumes of "Politique Positive," M. Comte revises and reelaborates the scientific and historical expositions of his first treatise. His object is to systematize (again to systematize) knowledge from the human or subjective point of view, the only one, he contends, from which a real synthesis is possible. For (he says) the knowledge attainable by us of the laws of the universe is at best fragmentary, and incapable of reduction to a real unity. An objective synthesis, the dream of Descartes and the best thinkers of old, is impossible. The laws of the real world are too numerous, and the manner of their working into one another too intricate, to be, as a general rule, correctly traced and represented by our reason. The only connecting principle in our knowledge is its relation to our wants, and it is upon that we must found our systematization. The answer to this is, first, that there is no necessity for an universal synthesis; and secondly, that the same arguments may be used against the possibility of a complete subjective, as of a complete objective systematization. A subjective synthesis must consist in the arrangement and co-ordination of all useful knowledge, on the basis of its relation to human wants and interests. But those wants and interests are, like the laws of the universe, extremely multifarious, and the order of preference among them in all their different gradations (for it varies according to the degree of each) cannot be cast into precise general propositions. M. Comte's subjective synthesis consists only in eliminating from the sciences everything that he deems useless, and presenting as far as possible every theoretical investigation as the solution of a practical problem. To this, however, he cannot consistently adhere; for, in every science, the theoretic truths are much more closely connected with one another than with the human purposes which they eventually serve, and can only be made to cohere in the intellect by being, to a great degree, presented as if they were truths of pure reason, irrespective of any practical application.

There are many things eminently characteristic of M. Comte's second career, in this revision of the results of his first. Under the head of Biology, and for the better combination of that science with Sociology and Ethics, he found that he required a new system of Phrenology, being justly dissatisfied with that of Gall and his successors. Accordingly he set about constructing one *è priori*, grounded on the best enumeration and classification he could make of the elementary faculties of our intellectual, moral, and animal nature; to each of which he assigned an hypothetical place in the skull, the most conformable that he could to the few positive facts on the subject which he considered as established, and to the general presumption that functions which react strongly on one another must have their organs adjacent: leaving the localities avowedly to be hereafter verified, by anatomical and inductive investigation. There is considerable merit in this attempt, though it is liable to obvious criticisms, of the same nature as his own upon Gall. But the characteristic thing is, that while presenting all this as hypothesis waiting for verification, he could not have taken its truth more completely for granted if the verification had been made. In all that he afterwards wrote, every detail of his theory of the brain is as unhesitatingly asserted, and as confidently built upon, as any other doctrine of science. This is his first great attempt in the "Subjective Method," which, originally meaning only the subordination of the pursuit of truth to human uses, had already come to mean drawing truth itself from the fountain of his own mind. He had become, on the one hand, almost indifferent to proof, provided he attained theoretic coherency, and on the other, serenely confident that even the guesses which originated with himself could not but come out true.

There is one point in his later view of the sciences, which appears to us a decided improvement on his earlier. He adds to the six fundamental sciences of his original scale, a seventh under the name of Morals, forming the highest step of the ladder, immediately after Sociology: remarking that it might, with still greater propriety, be termed Anthropology, being the science of individual human nature, a study, when rightly understood, more special and complicated than even that of Society. For it is obliged to take into consideration the diversities of constitution and temperament (la réaction cérébrale des viscères végétatifs) the effects of which, still very imperfectly understood, are highly important in the individual, but in the theory of society may be neglected, because, differing in different persons, they neutralize one another on the large scale. This is a remark worthy of M. Comte in his best days; and the science thus conceived is, as he says, the true scientific foundation of the art of Morals (and indeed of the art of human life), which, therefore, may, both philosophically and didactically, be properly combined with it.

His philosophy of general history is recast, and in many respects changed; we cannot but say, greatly for the worse. He gives much greater development than before to the Fetishistic, and to what he terms the Theocratic, periods. To the Fetishistic view of nature he evinces a partiality, which appears strange in a Positive philosopher. But the reason is that Fetish-worship is a religion of the feelings, and not at all of the intelligence. He regards it as cultivating universal love: as a practical fact it cultivates much rather universal fear. He looks upon Fetishism as much more akin to Positivism than any of the forms of Theology, inasmuch as these consider matter as inert, and moved only by forces, natural and supernatural, exterior to itself: while Fetishism resembles Positivism in conceiving matter as spontaneously active, and errs only by not distinguishing activity from life. As if the superstition of the Fetishist consisted only in believing that the objects which produce the phaenomena of nature involuntarily, produce them voluntarily. The Fetishist thinks not merely that his Fetish is alive, but that it can help him in war, can cure him of diseases, can grant him prosperity, or afflict him with all the contrary evils. Therein consists the lamentable effect of Fetishism—its degrading and prostrating influence on the feelings and conduct, its conflict with all genuine experience, and antagonism to all real knowledge of nature.

M. Comte had also no small sympathy with the Oriental theocracies, as he calls the sacerdotal castes, who indeed often deserved it by their early services to intellect and civilization; by the aid they gave to the establishment of regular government, the valuable though empirical knowledge they accumulated, and the height to which they helped to carry some of the useful arts. M. Comte admits that they became oppressive, and that the prolongation of their ascendancy came to be incompatible with further improvement. But he ascribes this to their having arrogated to themselves the temporal government, which, so far as we have any authentic information, they never did. The reason why the sacerdotal corporations became oppressive, was because they were organized: because they attempted the "unity" and "systematization" so dear to M. Comte, and allowed no science and no speculation, except with their leave and under their direction. M. Comte's sacerdotal order, which, in his system, has all the power that ever they had, would be oppressive in the same manner; with no variation but that which arises from the altered state of society and of the human mind.

M. Comte's partiality to the theocracies is strikingly contrasted with his dislike of the Greeks, whom as a people he thoroughly detests, for their undue addiction to intellectual speculation, and considers to have been, by an inevitable fatality, morally sacrificed to the formation of a few great scientific intellects,—principally Aristotle, Archimedes, Apollonius, and Hipparchus. Any one who knows Grecian history as it can now be known, will be amazed at M. Comte's travestie of it, in which the vulgarest historical prejudices are accepted and exaggerated, to illustrate the mischiefs of intellectual culture left to its own guidance.

There is no need to analyze further M. Comte's second view of universal history. The best chapter is that on the Romans, to whom, because they were greater in practice than in theory, and for centuries worked together in obedience to a social sentiment (though only that of their country's aggrandizement), M. Comte is as favourably affected, as he is inimical to all but a small selection of eminent thinkers among the Greeks. The greatest blemish in this chapter is the idolatry of Julius Caesar, whom M. Comte regards as one of the most illustrious characters in history, and of the greatest practical benefactors of mankind. Caesar had many eminent qualities, but what he did to deserve such praise we are at a loss to discover, except subverting a free government: that merit, however, with M. Comte, goes a great way. It did not, in his former days, suffice to rehabilitate Napoleon, whose name and memory he regarded with a bitterness highly honourable to himself, and whose career he deemed one of the greatest calamities in modern history. But in his later writings these sentiments are considerably mitigated: he regards Napoleon as a more estimable "dictator" than Louis Philippe, and thinks that his greatest error was re-establishing the Academy of Sciences! That this should be said by M. Comte, and said of Napoleon, measures the depth to which his moral standard had fallen.

The last volume which he published, that on the Philosophy of Mathematics, is in some respects a still sadder picture of intellectual degeneracy than those which preceded it. After the admirable résumé of the subject in the first volume of his first great work, we expected something of the very highest order when he returned to the subject for a more thorough treatment of it. But, being the commencement of a Synthèse Subjective, it contains, as might be expected, a great deal that is much more subjective than mathematical. Nor of this do we complain: but we little imagined of what nature this subjective matter was to be. M. Comte here joins together the two ideas, which, of all that he has put forth, are the most repugnant to the fundamental principles of Positive Philosophy. One of them is that on which we have just commented, the assimilation between Positivism and Fetishism. The other, of which we took notice in a former article, was the "liberté facultative" of shaping our scientific conceptions to gratify the demands not solely of objective truth, but of intellectual and aesthetic suitability. It would be an excellent thing, M. Comte thinks, if science could be deprived of its *sécheresse*, and directly associated with sentiment. Now it is impossible to prove that the external world, and the bodies composing it, are not endowed with feeling, and voluntary agency. It is therefore highly desirable that we should educate ourselves into imagining that they are. Intelligence it will not do to invest them with, for some distinction must be maintained between simple activity and life. But we may suppose that they feel what is done to them, and desire and will what they themselves do. Even intelligence, which we must deny to them in the present, may be attributed to them in the past. Before man existed, the earth, at that time an intelligent being, may have exerted "its physico-chemical activity so as to improve the astronomical order by changing its principal coefficients. Our planet may be supposed to have rendered its orbit less excentric, and thereby more habitable, by planning a long series of explosions, analogous to those from which, according to the best hypotheses, comets proceed. Judiciously reproduced, similar shocks may have rendered the inclination of the earth's axis better adapted to the future wants of the Grand Etre. *A fortiori* the Earth may have modified its own figure, which is only beyond our intervention because our spiritual ascendancy has not at its disposal a sufficient material force." The like may be conceived as having been done by each of the other planets, in concert, possibly, with the Earth and with one another. "In proportion as each planet improved its own condition, its life exhausted itself by excess of innervation; but with the consolation of rendering its self-devotion more efficacious, when the extinction of its special functions, first animal, and finally vegetative, reduced it to the universal attributes of feeling and activity."[25] This stuff, though he calls it fiction, he soon after speaks of as belief (croyance), to be greatly recommended, as at once satisfying our natural curiosity, and "perfecting our unity" (again unity!) "by supplying the gaps in our scientific notions with poetic fictions, and developing sympathetic emotions and aesthetic inspirations: the world being conceived as aspiring to second mankind in ameliorating the universal order under the impulse of the Grand Etre." And he obviously intends that we should be trained to make these fantastical inventions permeate all our associations, until we are incapable of conceiving the world and Nature apart from them, and they become equivalent to, and are in fact transformed into, real beliefs.

Wretched as this is, it is singularly characteristic of M. Comte's later mode of thought. A writer might be excused for introducing into an avowed work of fancy this dance of the planets, and conception of an animated Earth. If finely executed, he might even be admired for it. No one blames a poet for ascribing feelings, purposes, and human propensities to flowers. Because a conception might be interesting, and perhaps edifying, in a poem, M. Comte would have it imprinted on the inmost texture of every human mind in ordinary prose. If the imagination were not taught its prescribed lesson equally with the reason, where would be Unity? "It is important that the domain of fiction should become as *systematic* as that of demonstration, in order that their mutual harmony may be conformable to their respective destinations, both equally directed towards the continual increase of *unity*, personal and social."[26]

Nor is it enough to have created the Grand Fétiche (so he actually proposes to call the Earth), and to be able to include it and all concrete existence in our adoration along with the Grand Etre. It is necessary also to extend Positivist Fetishism to purely abstract existence; to "animate" the laws as well as the facts of nature. It is not sufficient to have made physics sentimental, mathematics must be made so too. This does not at first seem easy; but M. Comte finds the means of accomplishing it. His plan is, to make Space also an object of adoration, under the name of the Grand Milieu, and consider it as the representative of Fatality in general. "The final *unity* disposes us to cultivate sympathy by developing our gratitude to whatever serves the Grand Etre. It must dispose us to venerate the Fatality on which reposes the whole aggregate of our existence." We should conceive this Fatality as having a fixed seat, and that seat must be considered to be Space, which should be conceived as possessing feeling, but not activity or intelligence. And in our abstract speculations we should imagine all our conceptions as located in free Space. Our images of all sorts, down to our geometrical diagrams, and even our ciphers and algebraic symbols, should always be figured to ourselves as written in space, and not on paper or any other material substance. M. Comte adds that they should be conceived as green on a white ground.

We cannot go on any longer with this. In spite of it all, the volume on mathematics is full of profound thoughts, and will be very suggestive to those who take up the subject after M. Comte. What deep meaning there is, for example, in the idea that the infinitesimal calculus is a conception analogous to the corpuscular hypothesis in physics; which last M. Comte has always considered as a logical artifice; not an opinion respecting matters of fact. The assimilation, as it seems to us, throws a flood of light on both conceptions; on the physical one still more than the mathematical. We might extract many ideas of similar, though none perhaps of equal, suggestiveness. But mixed with these, what pitiable *niaiseries*! One of his great points is the importance of the "moral and intellectual properties of numbers." He cultivates a superstitious reverence for some of them. The first three are sacred, *les nombres sacrés*: One being the type of all Synthesis, Two of all Combination, which he now says *is* always binary (in his first treatise he only said that we may usefully represent it to ourselves as being so), and Three of all Progression, which not only requires three terms, but as he now maintains, never ought to have any more. To these sacred numbers all our mental operations must be made, as far as possible, to adjust themselves. Next to them, he has a great partiality for the number seven; for these whimsical reasons: "Composed of two progressions followed by a synthesis, or of one progression between two couples, the number seven, coming next after the sum of the three sacred numbers, determines the largest group which we can distinctly imagine. Reciprocally, it marks the limit of the divisions which we can directly conceive in a magnitude of any kind." The number seven, therefore, must be foisted in wherever possible, and among other things, is to be made the basis of numeration, which is hereafter to be septimal instead of decimal: producing all the inconvenience of a change of system, not only without getting rid of, but greatly aggravating, the disadvantages of the existing one. But then, he says, it is absolutely necessary that the basis of numeration should be a prime number. All other people think it absolutely necessary that it should not, and regard the present basis as only objectionable in not being divisible enough. But M. Comte's puerile predilection for prime numbers almost passes belief. His reason is that they are the type of irreductibility: each of them is a kind of ultimate arithmetical fact. This, to any one who knows M. Comte in his later aspects, is amply sufficient. Nothing can exceed his delight in anything which says to the human mind, Thus far shalt thou go and no farther. If prime numbers are precious, doubly prime numbers are doubly so; meaning those which are not only themselves prime numbers, but the number which marks their place in the series of prime numbers is a prime number. Still greater is the dignity of trebly prime numbers; when the number marking the place of this second number is also prime. The number thirteen fulfils these conditions: it is a prime number, it is the seventh prime number, and seven is the fifth prime number. Accordingly he has an outrageous partiality to the number thirteen. Though one of the most inconvenient of all small numbers, he insists on introducing it everywhere.

These strange conceits are connected with a highly characteristic example of M. Comte's frenzy for regulation. He cannot bear that anything should be left unregulated: there ought to be no such thing as hesitation; nothing should remain arbitrary, for *l'arbitraire* is always favourable to egoism. Submission to artificial prescriptions is as indispensable as to natural laws, and he boasts that under the reign of sentiment, human life may be made equally, and even more, regular than the courses of the stars. But the great instrument of exact regulation for the details of life is numbers: fixed numbers, therefore, should be introduced into all our conduct. M. Comte's first application of this system was to the correction of his own literary style. Complaint had been made, not undeservedly, that in his first great work, especially in the latter part of it, the sentences and paragraphs were long, clumsy, and involved. To correct this fault, of which he was aware, he imposed on himself the following rules. No sentence was to exceed two lines of his manuscript, equivalent to five of print. No paragraph was to consist of more than seven sentences. He further applied to his prose writing the rule of French versification which forbids a *hiatus*(the concourse of two vowels), not allowing it to himself even at the break between two sentences or two paragraphs; nor did he permit himself ever to use the same word twice, either in the same sentence or in two consecutive sentences, though belonging to different paragraphs: with the exception of the monosyllabic auxiliaries.[27] All this is well enough, especially the first two precepts, and a good way of breaking through a bad habit. But M. Comte persuaded himself that any arbitrary restriction, though in no way emanating from, and therefore necessarily disturbing, the natural order and proportion of the thoughts, is a benefit in itself, and tends to improve style. If it renders composition vastly more difficult, he rejoices at it, as tending to confine writing to superior minds. Accordingly, in the Synthèse Subjective, he institutes the following "plan for all compositions of importance." "Every volume really capable of forming a distinct treatise" should consist of "seven chapters, besides the introduction and the conclusion; and each of these should be composed of three parts." Each third part of a chapter should be divided into "seven sections, each composed of seven groups of sentences, separated by the usual break of line. Normally formed, the section offers a central group of seven sentences, preceded and followed by three groups of five: the first section of each part reduces to three sentences three of its groups, symmetrically placed; the last section gives seven sentences to each of its extreme groups. These rules of composition make prose approach to the regularity of poetry, when combined with my previous reduction of the maximum length of a sentence to two manuscript or five printed lines, that is, 250 letters." "Normally constructed, great poems consist of thirteen cantos, decomposed into parts, sections, and groups like my chapters, saving the complete equality of the groups and of the sections." "This difference of structure between volumes of poetry and of philosophy is more apparent than real, for the introduction and the conclusion of a poem should comprehend six of its thirteen cantos," leaving, therefore, the cabalistic numeber seven for the body of the poem. And all this regulation not being sufficiently meaningless, fantastic, and oppressive, he invents an elaborate system for compelling each of his sections and groups to begin with a letter of the alphabet, determined beforehand, the letters being selected so as to compose words having "a synthetic or sympathetic signification," and as close a relation as possible to the section or part to which they are appropriated.

Others may laugh, but we could far rather weep at this melancholy decadence of a great intellect. M. Comte used to reproach his early English admirers with maintaining the "conspiracy of silence" concerning his later performances. The reader can now judge whether such reticence is not more than sufficiently explained by tenderness for his fame, and a conscientious fear of bringing undeserved discredit on the noble speculations of his early career.

M. Comte was accustomed to consider Descartes and Leibnitz as his principal precursors, and the only great philosophers (among many thinkers of high philosophic capacity) in modern times. It was to their minds that he considered his own to bear the nearest resemblance. Though we have not so lofty an opinion of any of the three as M. Comte had, we think the assimilation just: thes were, of all recorded thinkers, the two who bore most resemblance to M. Comte. They were like him in earnestness, like him, though scarcely equal to him, in confidence in themselves; they had the same extraordinary power of concatenation and co-ordination; they enriched human knowledge with great truths and great conceptions of method; they were, of all great scientific thinkers, the most consistent, and for that reason often the most absurd, because they shrank from no consequences, however contrary to common sense, to which their premises appeared to lead. Accordingly their names have come down to us associated with grand thoughts, with most important discoveries, and also with some of the most extravagantly wild and ludicrously absurd conceptions and theories which ever were solemnly propounded by thoughtful men. "We think M. Comte as great as either of these philosophers, and hardly more extravagant. Were we to speak our whole mind, we should call him superior to them: though not intrinsically, yet by the exertion of equal intellectual power in a more advanced state of human preparation; but also in an age less tolerant of palpable absurdities, and to which those he has committed, if not in themselves greater, at least appear more ridiculous.

THE END.

FOOTNOTES:

[1] See the Chapter on Efficient Causes in Reid's "Essays on the Active Powers," which is avowedly grounded on Newton's ideas.

[2] Mr Herbert Spencer, who also distinguishes between abstract and concrete sciences, employs the terms in a different sense from that explained above. He calls a science abstract when its truths are merely ideal; when, like the truths of geometry, they are not exactly true of real things—or, like the so-called law of inertia (the persistence in direction and velocity of a motion once impressed) are "involved" in experience but never actually seen in it, being always more or less completely frustrated. Chemistry and biology he includes, on the contrary, among concrete sciences, because chemical combinations and decompositions, and the physiological action of tissues, do actually take place (as our senses testify) in the manner in which the scientific

propositions state them to take place. We will not discuss the logical or philological propriety of either use of the terms abstract and concrete, in which twofold point of view very few of the numerous acceptations of these words are entirely defensible: but of the two distinctions M. Comte's answers to by far the deepest and most vital difference. Mr Spencer's is open to the radical objection, that it classifies truths not according to their subject-matter or their mutual relations, but according to an unimportant difference in the manner in which we come to know them. Of what consequence is it that the law of inertia (considered as an exact truth) is not generalized from our direct perceptions, but inferred by combining with the movements which we see, those which we should see if it were not for the disturbing causes? In either case we are equally certain that it *is* an exact truth: for every dynamical law is perfectly fulfilled even when it seems to be counteracted. There must, we should think, be many truths in physiology (for example) which are only known by a similar indirect process; and Mr Spencer would hardly detach these from the body of the science, and call them abstract and the remainder concrete.

[3] Système de Politique Positive, ii. 36.

[4] The strongest case which Mr Spencer produces of a scientifically ascertained law, which, though belonging to a later science, was necessary to the scientific formation of one occupying an earlier place in M. Comte's series, is the law of the accelerating force of gravity; which M. Comte places in Physics, but without which the Newtonian theory of the celestial motions could not have been discovered, nor could even now be proved. This fact, as is judiciously remarked by M. Littré, is not valid against the plan of M. Comte's classification, but discloses a slight error in the detail. M. Comte should not have placed the laws of terrestrial gravity under Physics. They are part of the general theory of gravitation, and belong to astronomy. Mr Spencer has hit one of the weak points in M. Comte's scientific scale; weak however only because left unguarded. Astronomy, the second of M. Comte's abstract sciences, answers to his own definition of a concrete science. M. Comte however was only wrong in overlooking a distinction. There *is* an abstract science of astronomy, namely, the theory of gravitation, which would equally agree with and explain the facts of a totally different solar system from the one of which our earth forms a part. The actual facts of our own system, the dimensions, distances, velocities, temperatures, physical constitution, &c., of the sun, earth, and planets, are properly the subject of a concrete science, similar to natural history; but the concrete is more inseparably united to the abstract science than in any other case, since the few celestial facts really accessible to us are nearly all required for discovering and proving the law of gravitation as an universal property of bodies, and have therefore an indispensable place in the abstract science as its fundamental

data.

[5] The only point at which the general principle of the series fails in its application, is the subdivision of Physics; and there, as the subordination of the different branches scarcely exists, their order is of little consequence. Thermology, indeed, is altogether an exception to the principle of decreasing generality, heat, as Mr Spencer truly says being as universal as gravitation. But the place of Thermology is marked out, within certain narrow limits, by the ends of the classification, though not by its principle. The desideratum is, that every science should precede those which cannot be scientifically constitute or rationally studied until it is known. It is as a means to this end, that the arrangement of the phaenomena in the order of their dependence on one another is important. Now, though heat is as universal a phaenomenon as any which external nature presents, its laws do not affect, in any manner important to us, the phaenomena of Astronomy, and operate in the other branches of Physics only as slight modifying agencies, the consideration of which may be postponed to a rather advanced stage. But the phaenomena of Chemistry and Biology depend on them often for their very existence. The ends of the classification require therefore that Thermology should precede Chemistry and Biology, but do not demand that it should be thrown farther back. On the other hand, those same ends, in another point of view, require that it should be subsequent to Astronomy, for reasons not of doctrine but of method: Astronomy being the best school of the true art of interpreting Nature, by which Thermology profits like other sciences, but which it was ill adapted to originate.

[6] The philosophy of the subject is perhaps nowhere so well expressed as in the "Système de Politique Positive" (iii. 41). "Conçu logiquement, l'ordre suivant lequel nos principales théories accomplissent l'évolution fondamentale résulte nécessairement de leur dépendance mutuelle. Toutes les sciences peuvent, sans doute, être ébauchées à la fois: leur usage pratique exige même cette culture simultanée. Mais elle ne peut concerner que les inductions propres à chaque classe de spéculations. Or cet essor inductif ne saurait fournir des principes suffisants qu'envers les plus simples études. Partout ailleurs, ils ne peuvent être établis qu'en subordonnant chaque genre d'inductions scientifiques à l'ensemble des déductions emanées des domaines moins compliqués, et dès-lors moins dépendants. Ainsi nos diverses théories reposent dogmatiquement les unes sur les autres, suivant un ordre invariable, qui doit régler historiquement leur avénement décisif, les plus indépendantes ayant toujours dû se développer plus tôt."

[7] "Science," says Mr Spencer in his "Genesis," "while purely inductive is purely qualitative.... All quantitative prevision is reached deductively; induction can achieve only qualitative prevision." Now, if we remember that the very first accurate quantitative law of physical phaenomena ever established, the

law of the accelerating force of gravity, was discovered and proved by Galileo partly at least by experiment; that the quantitative laws on which the whole theory of the celestial motions is grounded, were generalized by Kepler from direct comparison of observations; that the quantitative law of the condensation of gases by pressure, the law of Boyle and Mariotte, was arrived at by direct experiment; that the proportional quantities in which every known substance combines chemically with every other, were ascertained by innumerable experiments, from which the general law of chemical equivalents, now the ground of the most exact quantitative previsions, was an inductive generalization; we must conclude that Mr Spencer has committed himself to a general proposition, which a very slight consideration of truths perfectly known to him would have shown to be unsustainable.

Again, in the very pamphlet in which Mr Spencer defends himself against the supposition of being a disciple of M. Comte ("The Classification of the Sciences," p. 37), he speaks of "M. Comte's adherent, Mr Buckle." Now, except in the opinion common to both, that history may be made a subject of science, the speculations of these two thinkers are not only different, but run in different channels, M. Comte applying himself principally to the laws of evolution common to all mankind, Mr Buckle almost exclusively to the diversities: and it may be affirmed without presumption, that they neither saw the same truths, nor fell into the same errors, nor defended their opinions, either true or erroneous, by the same arguments. Indeed, it is one of the surprising things in the case of Mr Buckle as of Mr Spencer, that being a man of kindred genius, of the same wide range of knowledge, and devoting himself to speculations of the same kind, he profited so little by M. Comte.

These oversights prove nothing against the general accuracy of Mr Spencer's acquirements. They are mere lapses of inattention, such as thinkers who attempt speculations requiring that vast multitudes of facts should be kept in recollection at once, can scarcely hope always to avoid.

[8] We refer particularly to the mystical metaphysics connected with the negative sign, imaginary quantities, infinity and infinitesimals, &c., all cleared up and put on a rational footing in the highly philosophical treatises of Professor De Morgan.

[9] Those who wish to see this idea followed out, are referred to "A System of Logic, Ratiocinative and Inductive." It is not irrelevant to state that M. Comte, soon after the publication of that work, expressed, both in a letter (published in M. Littré's volume) and in print, his high approval of it (especially of the Inductive part) as a real contribution to the construction of the Positive Method. But we cannot discover that he was indebted to it for a single idea, or that it influenced, in the smallest particular, the course of his subsequent speculations.

[10] The force, however, of this last consideration has been much weakened

by the progress of discovery since M. Comte left off studying chemistry; it being now probable that most if not all substances, even elementary, are susceptible of *allotropic* forms; as in the case of oxygen and ozone, the two forms of phosphorus, &c.

[11] Thus; by considering prussic acid as a compound of hydrogen and cyanogen rather than of hydrogen and the elements of cyanogen (carbon and nitrogen), it is assimilated to a whole class of acid compounds between hydrogen and other substances, and a reason is thus found for its agreeing in their acid properties.

[12] According to Sir William Hamilton, as many as six; but numerical precision in such matters is out of the question, and it is probable that different minds have the power in different degrees.

[13] Or, as afterwards corrected by him, the appetites and emotions, the active capacities, and the intellectual faculties; "le coeur," "le caractère," and "l'esprit."

[14] M. Littré, who, though a warm admirer, and accepting the position of a disciple of M. Comte, is singularly free from his errors, makes the equally ingenious and just remark, that Political Economy corresponds in social science to the theory of the nutritive functions in biology, which M. Comte, with all good physiologists, thinks it not only permissible but a great and fundamental improvement to treat, in the first place, separately, as the necessary basis of the higher branches of the science: although the nutritive functions can no more be withdrawn *in fact* from the influence of the animal and human attributes, than the economical phaenomena of society from that of the political and moral.

[15] Indeed his claim to be the creator of Sociology does not extend to this branch of the science; on the contrary, he, in a subsequent work, expressly declares that the real founder of it was Aristotle, by whom the theory of the conditions of social existence was carried as far towards perfection as was possible in the absence of any theory of Progress. Without going quite this length, we think it hardly possible to appreciate too highly the merit of those early efforts, beyond which little progress had been made, until a very recent period, either in ethical or in political science.

[16] It is due to them both to say, that he continued to express, in letters which have been published, a high opinion of her, both morally and intellectually; and her persistent and strong concern for his interests and his fame is attested both by M. Littré and by his own correspondence.

[17] "Of the Classification of the Sciences," pp. 37, 38.

[18] In the case of Egypt we admit that there may be cited against us the authority of Plato, in whose Politicus it is said that the king of Egypt must be a member of the priestly caste, or if by usurpation a member of any other caste acquired the sovereignty he must be initiated with the sacerdotal order.

But Plato was writing of a state of things which already belonged to the past; nor have we any assurance that his information on Egyptian institutions was authentic and accurate. Had the king been necessarily or commonly a member of the priestly order, it is most improbable that the careful Herodotus, of whose comprehensive work an entire book was devoted to a minute account of Egypt and its institutions, and who collected his information from Egyptian priests in the country itself, would have been ignorant of a part so important, and tending so much to exalt the dignity of the priesthood, who were much more likely to affirm it falsely to Plato than to withhold the knowledge of it if true from Heredotus. Not only is Herodotus silent respecting any such law or custom, but he thinks it needful to mention that in one particular instance the king (by name Sethôs) was a priest, which he would scarcely have done if this had been other than an exceptional case. It is likely enough that a king of Egypt would learn the hieratic character, and would not suffer any of the mysteries of law or religion which were in the keeping of the priests to be withheld from him; and this was very probably all the foundation which existed for the assertion of the Eleatic stranger in Plato's dialogue.

[19] Mill, History of British India, book ii. chap. iii.

[20] At a somewhat later period M. Comte drew up what he termed a Positivist Calendar, in which every day was dedicated to some benefactor of humanity (generally with the addition of a similar but minor luminary, to be celebrated in the room of his principal each bissextile year). In this no kind of human eminence, really useful, is omitted, except that which is merely negative and destructive. On this principle (which is avowed) the French *philosophes* as such are excluded, those only among them being admitted who, like Voltaire and Diderot, had claims to admission on other grounds: and the Protestant religious reformers are left out entirely, with the curious exception of George Fox—who is included, we presume, in consideration of his Peace principles.

[21] He goes still further and deeper in a subsequent work. "L'art ramène doucement à la réalite les contemplations trop abstraites du théoricien, tandis qu'il pousse noblement le praticien aux speculations désinteressées." Système de Politique Positive, i. 287.

[22] 1. *Système de Politique Positive, ou Traité de Sociologie, instituant la Religion de l'Humanité.* 4 vols. 8vo. Paris: 1851—1854.

2. *Catéchisme Positiviste, ou Sommaire Exposition de la Religion Universelle, en onze Entretiens Systématiques entre une Femme et un Prêtre de l'Humanité.* 1 vol. 12mo. Paris: 1852.

3. *Appel aux Conservateurs.* Paris: 1855 (brochure).

4. *Synthèse Subjective, ou Système Universel des Conceptions propres à l'Etat Normal de l'Humanité.* Tome Premier, contenant le Système de Logique Positive, ou

Traité de Philosophie Mathématique. 8vo. Paris: 1856.

5. *Auguste Comte et la Philosophie Positive.* Par E. LITTRE. 1 vol. 8vo. Paris: 1863.

6. *Exposition Abrégée et Populaire de la Philosophie et de la Religion Positives.* PAR CÉLESTIN DE BLIGNIÈRES, ancien élève de l'Ecole Polytechnique. 1 vol. 12mo. Paris: 1857.

7. *Notice sur l'Oeuvre et sur la Vie d'Auguste Comte.* Par le DOCTEUR ROBINET, son Médecin, et l'un de ses treize Exécuteurs Testamentaires. 1 vol. 8vo. Paris: 1860.

[23] Système de Politique Positive, iv. 100.
[24] See Sir John Herschel's Outlines of Astronomy, § 319.
[25] Synthèse Subjective, pp. 10, 11.
[26] Synthèse Subjective, pp. 11, 12.

Printed in Great Britain
by Amazon.co.uk, Ltd.,
Marston Gate.